THE Final Days OF JESUS

Published by Sacred Holidays. © 2019 Sacred Holidays

ISBN 978-0-9982268-4-2

Unless otherwise noted, all Scripture quotations are from the ESV Study Bible
The Holy Bible, English Standard Version® (ESV®)
Copyright © 2001 by Crossway, a publishing ministry of Good News Publishers.

ESV® Permanent Text Edition® (2016)

Cover and interior design: Megan Sjuts | Building 07 (www.building07.com)
Edited by Molly Parker (mollyjeanparker.com)

To order additional copies of this resource:
Visit the online shop: www.sacredholidays.com/shop

To order in bulk at a discounted rate (orders over 50 studies) for churches, bookstores, ministries or non-profits, contact hello@sacredholidays.com.

If you know someone who is unable to afford this study and you are unable to purchase it for him or her, please see the Discounts page under the Lent tab at www.sacredholidays.com.

Printed in the United States of America

Sacred Holidays, P.O. BOX 131476, Spring, Texas, 77381

I'm not sure if we are real life friends, but I'm pretty sure I'd want to be. Already, I know you are brave. I mean, who picks up a seven-and-a-half-week Bible study?! You are crazy, and I love me some crazy. I also know you want Jesus desperately, like really want to know Him. Oh, friend, you will. If I've ever felt confident about that statement with a study, it's this one. This is all about Him and living out the things that mattered most to Him.

This study is for the woman who's been in Bible study since she could read and write (and we won't say how many decades have passed since that started). It's for the woman who's never picked up a Bible, much less a Bible study. This study is for everyone in between—the woman who picks up a study and never finishes, the woman who started the year off with the best of intentions, the woman who loves His Word with every fiber of her being. Whichever woman you are, you're welcome here. This is for the woman whose life is going pretty good, other than a deep lack of meaning. This is for the woman who is exhausted from pouring herself out for others so often. This is for the woman who prayed as she clicked to get this study, "Lord, this is my last attempt to seek You." It's for the woman who could not be more excited for the things God is doing in and through her. Whichever woman you are, you're welcome here.

More than you are welcome here, you are welcome with Jesus. It's what I love about Him most—how He's always about others yet steady in His own identity. His whole life, as we will see, was about others—their healing, their hope, their correction, their identity. He never wavered, not once. He showed His humanity and was vulnerable, but let's not mistake that for weakness. Our God is enough for whatever you bring Him today.

Jesus's final days on earth were beautiful and heart wrenching. We're going to journey with Him. Lean in. Give this study everything you have. The format is different than any study we've put out before or that I've personally done, so be sure to check out the Start Here section.

Much love! Mean it.

Becky Kiser

P.S. Also, can I shamelessly plug social media? I really like it and I know (most of) you do too. I'm sure some of you might give it up for Lent, and if you do, then stop reading the rest of this page. Social media does a lot of damage to us as women. Am I right? But one thing that's wildly beautiful is how it connects us in ways we might not share without it. I love seeing your faces. I wish we could all gather in my living room each week, as I do with women locally during our studies. I want to hear your stories and see pics of your days. I love it even more when you all start to fall in love with one another too. Let's cheer each other on this Lent. We are a sisterhood, a tribe. No drama allowed in our tribe, just love. Deal?

So join in and follow along and use #sacredholidays and tag @sacredholidays when you post about anything relevant. Don't forget get to join the SH Facebook Tribe page too! Please and thank you!

start here

how to use this study

Hooray—the study is starting! I know it's pretty typical to skip intro sections, but take the time as you'll likely find this study a little different from what you've done before. Know too, that if you ever have questions, you can email us anytime at hello@sacredholidays.com.

For many of you, studying God's Word comes second nature, and for others, it can be overwhelming. Knowing how to study God's Word and walk with Him are lacking in our current culture. We tend to take what others have learned, letting social media, podcasts, church, and books become our crutch. These things aren't bad, but they can't be the only places we take in God's Word. So let's study His Word—and His life—this Lent . . . for ourselves!

Now, let's chat about the study!

Pick Your Pace

We want you to choose your flow each week. With the exception of the first and last week, due to shortened weeks, you can expect the same amount of content. However, we do encourage you to do two things. First, stick with our weekly timeline to keep yourself on track. Second, do the light days on Sundays or to kick-off your week.

You have the freedom to schedule your week however you'd like, but be sure to set yourself up for success! Be realistic as you fill out your chart at the beginning of each week. And if you fall behind, pick up where you left off.

Trust the Spirit in you to lead you at your own pace, knowing that shame is not from your Father. I hate to put dates on study days because automatically our check-the-list selves take over. Enter with that come shame and failure, when we don't meet our standards. Fight this. Connecting with Jesus is not a check-the-box thing; it's only a connecting with Jesus thing. Man created Bible studies and calendars and checkbox lists, so give yourself some grace. Deal?

WEEK DAY	ITEM(S) TO DO	OBSTACLES	SOLUTIONS
SUN	Light all candles	Church, family day	Shower night before and lay out clothes for church, wake up early
MON	Ask for others and myself		
TUES	Yield to God	Full day with the girls, Teaching Bible Study	Make sure teaching lesson is prepped before Tuesday
WED	Sabbath	Get busy with To Dos	Mark off calendar. Shut office door. Turn phone to airplane mode.
THUR	Blow out first candle		
FRI	Faith and fruit	Not make the time for this w/ end of week.	Wake up early to do this before anyone else is up.
SAT	Get angry and make space	Weekend travel	Do this before going to bed. Oops—missed Thurs, do today too.

Weekly Candle Lighting & Light Focused Scripture Study

If you aren't familiar with Lent, then the process of Lent candles will be a little strange for you, but something I highly encourage! It's a simple practice and will remind you throughout the day of what you are preparing your heart for. I recommend placing your candles where you will see them often. Have some at home, but also consider having some at work. I have small, battery-operated candles that are safe (and cheap!) and great for work spaces or for those with littles at home.

Unlike Advent candles, Lent begins with all the candles lit—because the Light of the World has already come! Then as we near the Cross, each Sunday we blow out another candle. On Good Friday, we blow out the final candle and experience the darkness of Christ's death. Then on Easter Sunday we light all seven candles to celebrate the Light, which has defeated darkness forever!

> » *Where could you put your Lent candles so you see them often?*

Keep it simple. You will need seven candles, and they can be any size and any color.

> » *What supplies do you need? When can you go get them? Mark your calendar.*

Be sure to follow us on Facebook, as we will post instructional videos on the reason for Lent candles and how to use them.

Prayer Prompt to Start Each Session

Every day we start with prayer because learning to talk to our Father is a hard discipline. Fight the temptation to skip this prompt. I use the acronym PRAY and then pause to Wait and Listen.

PRAISE: Thank God for who He is and what He has done—in His Word and all around you.

REPENT: Confess sin—the things that separate us from Him.

ASK: Request things for others, for things going on in the world, or whatever else He brings to mind.

YIELD: Surrender yourself and anything going on in your life today to your Father.

WAIT AND LISTEN: Pause afterwards and listen to see if God speaks back to you. You won't likely hear an audible voice (I never have), but you will experience a knowing. The more you listen the more you will hear that voice in your heart, as the Holy Spirit speaks. And oftentimes we get our response the next time we open His Word!

You might prefer to grab a journal to write out your prayers if you need more space. Or you can pray without writing. I do a little bit of both—I jot down key words and then talk to the Father.

What Should I Do? Application

We can often rush off at the end of a time of Bible study. When we do this, we keep the knowledge of what we've learned in our heads and even our hearts, but don't let it go to our hands, mouths, or feet. Let's change that this year! After we have studied His Word, let's live out the command found in James 1:22, "Do not merely listen to the Word, and so deceive yourselves. Do what it says . . ."

This prompt is really centered on taking action on a truth you read about that day and applying it to your own life. The Lord might challenge you to start doing something, like waking up earlier to get in His Word or pray with more faith. He might correct you, asking you to stop doing something, like gossiping or judging a certain person or group.

There might be some days you have several things you need to do, and other days this stays blank—both are totally fine! The important thing is that you pause and ask the Lord if there is anything you should do.

Who Should I Tell? Challenge

While the What Should I Do application gets us thinking about areas we need to change in our lives, the Who Should I Tell challenge focuses more on sharing with others what God is teaching you. Don't worry, we aren't going to have you go knock on strangers' doors every day, or even any day for that matter. The intent is way more natural. After you've talked to your Father in prayer, studied His Word, become a doer of His Word, you are ready to tell others! Jesus's final command was to go and make disciples (Matthew 28). Because we love others, we should want to share what is true with them!

The problem is, this often makes us very uncomfortable. We don't want to offend, so we say nothing at all. We fear that sharing something others might not agree with is unloving, so we choose silence instead. Hear me, this is not the best way we can love them. If we really believe what God is teaching us is true, than we should share it with others.

Some days you will have something to tell, other days you won't. The point is that you slow down and ask the Father to give you a courageous heart and brave feet. You can do this!

At the end of each Scripture study day you will see these prompts:

WHAT SHOULD I DO?

How can you apply what you have heard today? (James 1:22)

WHO SHOULD I TELL?

What is something you can share about today? Who should you share this with?

Some people or groups to consider when when deciding who to tell each day:

- People you live with (i.e., family or roommates)
- Co-Workers
- Extended Family Members
- Friends
- Neighbors
- Strangers (look up when you are out and about)
- Social Media friends and followers

We have so many ways we can tell people: in person, text, phone call, email, or whatever way you communicate. You can also share more broadly by posting on social media. During seasons like Easter, many are more open to hearing these kinds of truths. We know this is true because churches are packed on Easter. They want to be a part of this story, many just don't know how to find their way to it. You can help tell them what is true about the Father.

"Go therefore and make disciples of all nations, baptizing them in the name of the Father and of the Son and of the Holy Spirit, teaching them to observe all that I have commanded you. And behold, I am with you always, to the end of the age."

Matthew 28:19-20

Prayer Days

One traditional aspect of Lent is to be very repentant and reflective, so we created space to do just that. You can combine this with a Bible study reading day, or it an be done on a day all by itself. Each week we will guide you and give you creative direction to experience prayer in different ways. You are welcome to follow this prompt exactly or do something else on these days. The hope is that you would focus more on prayer during this Lenten season.

Sabbath

There isn't a right or a wrong way to "do Sabbath." The intent with adding this is that we would simply lean into it a little bit more. Most of us struggle with Sabbath—we are a hurry and go society or a totally veg out, we live in those extremes. Instead, let's find ways to really rest and renew ourselves in the Lord. Try something new each week or do the same thing. We will give tips and ideas on social media!

Create a Sabbath action plan. Whether it is a full day or a set amount of hours, it matters to Him. Set aside the time and prepare for it!

I will enjoy Sabbath from __:__ __ AM/PM to __:__ __ AM/PM on _____.

» *In order to make time for Sabbath, I need to:*

Stay Connected

Research shows that when you do something with others, you are more likely to follow through and have better results. It's the reason why Weight Watchers, CrossFit, and all our friends online want us to join their fitness groups for just 30 days—when you do things with others, you are more likely to succeed.

You don't have to do this study alone! I love doing studies with other people for two main reasons: it forces me to stick with it, and I love learning what they have learned. Inevitably, when we start talking, someone will share something I didn't even see. Or their faith encourages me to push into Jesus more, instead of going after Him half-heartedly.

Here are a few ways you can stay connected with others:

#1: Join the Sacred Holidays Tribe (our private Facebook group). This is a great space to go when you want to connect with others who want the same thing out of Lent as you do. There, you can share what God has taught you that day, share prayer requests (we love messy and vulnerable), and be accepted just as you are.

> *» Go to facebook.com/groups/SacredHolidaysTribe to join and write "I joined" below:*

#2: Ask a few friends to join you! It's never too late because Amazon ships all the time, anytime, so people can join even in the last week (and they do)!

> *» Who are 2-5 friends you could text right now and ask to join you?*

#3: Host or co-host a group—we give you EVERYTHING you need to lead! If you are interested in hosting a group, check out our Group page on the Lent tab for all kinds of resources. We have a guide that provides tips for leading groups, both in person and online. Plus we provide weekly checklists and questions for group leaders, if you would like the extra support. Also, we have a private Facebook Group just for our Group leaders to share tips, prayer requests, and encouragement.

If you don't want to host a group, but you'd love to be in a group, check out our Group Page on the website to see if there is one near you.

Reflect + Commit

A seven-and-a-half-week Bible study is a little cray-cray. Now most are only four-five days long—and for good reason. I remember when I first became a Christian, Bible studies were about eight weeks long with many pages to flip through and Scripture to read. Perhaps research now shows that people rarely finished those studies, so they decided to make them easier. Maybe because their research showed that people didn't finish them and they wanted to make it easier to do it.

We aren't going for easy. We are going after Jesus.

Let's go after Him! As a life coach, I am a big believer in reflection and goal setting because it actually works. Take the time to do this reflection and commitment section. It might take around 30 minutes to complete. Don't let all the open space overwhelm you. When we take the time to learn from the past and make every effort to move forward in a beneficial way, then we have a great advantage to succeed.

REFLECT

» *How would you describe your relationship with the Lord right now? Be honest.*

» *How often do you spend focused time with Him—not rushed or on-the-go time, but still and focused time with Him. Some call this a "quiet time."*

» *What does studying the Word look like for you?*

» *What does prayer look like for you?*

» Why did you pick up this Lent Bible study?

» What do you hope to get out of it?

COMMIT

Our commitments are our yeses to God. A common misconception I see in the Church is the assumption that if it is about God then it should come easily. I'm not sure where we started believing this lie, but let me tell you that it is definitely a lie. I might even venture to say that things that are of God and will cause people to follow God more passionately will actually be a great struggle for us. Our enemy, the devil, would like nothing more than to cripple His followers during a season that should be all about Him.

Commit this time to Him. You are worth it. He is worth it.

I know we like to try to make things attainable, so we aim low so we can easily reach our target. Ladies, DO NOT deprive yourself or aim low in your pursuit of God. Don't give yourself so much grace that you miss out on Him. I have met very few women that couldn't actually make time with God a thing each day. Make Him a priority. Give Him your full attention and put Him ahead of every other item on the list. Also, there is NOTHING in Scripture that deems the morning hours more spiritual than any other time. Before kiddos, my best time to meet with the Lord was at night after my parents or my roommates were in bed. I was without distraction and didn't have to rush off anywhere. With kids, it's essential to wake up early (which I hate so very much), or I will be a wreck. Choose the time that is best and most realistic for you.

» How will you make time to do your Bible study each day?

» Write what time you will do your Bible study and where. Then set an alarm on your phone to go off each day at the time you set. I find it helpful to turn on the snooze feature so you have to hit snooze until you actually begin. Initial below once you've set your alarm.

What obstacles will prevent you from making this time a reality? List each one out below. Then write out your action plan.

OBSTACLES	WHAT CAN YOU DO ABOUT IT?

Write out a prayer to the Lord committing this study to Him. Make your promise of how you will meet with Him. Ask Him to help you keep that. Be brave in asking Him to move during this time!

Share this with someone and write their name(s) below. We do better in life when we live in community. Snap a pic of these pages and share them with a friend, or show them to a family member, or even share them on social media. The accountability will be good.

Fast

Fasting is a traditional part of Lent. We don't have the space or time to talk about all the reasons we fast. I highly encourage you to maybe do some research this next week on fasting. You don't have to be a scholar to get some clear answers. You can start by simply googling "What does the Bible say about fasting," or something like that. You can search verses on fasting as well to see accounts of fasting in Scripture.

We can be sure, though, that fasting has always been a part of the language and expectations for those following Christ. Fasting shows our own weaknesses and our dependencies on Christ. Fasting breaks our bondage to sinful things or things that aren't good for us.

There are many ways you can fast. Some people fast from food completely, some fast from certain things that they really love (as a sacrifice to the Lord), and others fast from things that keep them from the Lord. Regardless of what you choose, it should be something you don't really want to do. That's kinda the point.

» What are you going to fast from?

» Why are choosing this?

Join or Start a Group

If you want to get the very most out of this study, then gather some people and do it together. This is how Jesus lived—with others. He invited people in and up close. Let's do the same. It's not too late!

> *» Even though you are likely busy, do you think doing this study with others would benefit you? Would it help you stick with it better? Would it help you learn more?*

> *» What would be the best way for you to do this with others? (Some groups meet weekly in person, others every other week. Some groups start a Facebook group, others just text each other throughout the Lent season. And there are many churches that host groups for women each season too.)*

> *» Which friends could you ask to do this study with you?*

Send them a quick text and invite them to join you. Trust me, you will NOT regret it. This past Advent I really wanted to keep things simple and I almost didn't open up my home. You know what? It actually forced me to keep things simple. When I invited people into the journey, it held me to walk it out. I feel confident it can be the same for you.

Y'all can meet in person or even online. We have several groups that are friends all over the nation and they start a private Facebook Group and support one another all week and do some Facebook Lives to visually connect. Do whatever works for you!

SIGN YOUR GROUP UP AND JOIN THE PRIVATE FACEBOOK GROUP FOR SUPPORT!

If you are ready to start a group, we have lots of tips and support for you! Head over to the Groups tab on the website and sign your group up. You will be given access to our private Facebook group for our leaders, as well as contact with our support team member for groups. You will be fully resourced with ideas on how to best start your group, as well as weekly support for discussion and keeping momentum going in your group!

weekly plan

WEEK DAY	✓	ITEM(S) TO DO	OBSTACLES	SOLUTIONS
SUN				
MON				
TUES				
WED				
THUR				
FRI				
SAT				

FASTING

This week I will fast from:

_____

I am fasting from this because:

_____

In order to keep this fast, I need to:

_____

Week 1

Praise God, the Light of the World! (Light All Candles)

Justice Through Repentence

Ask for Others and Yourself

Yield to God

Sabbath

Praise God, the Light of the World!

PRAISE GOD.

_____

_____

_____

_____

_____

This first week we are going to break apart our daily prayer prompt because Lent is traditionally known as a season of prayer and repentance. We will start every day the same way: Praising God, Repenting of Sin, Asking for Others + Ourselves, Yielding to God, then Waiting and Listening. We do this to deepen our relationship with God. A relationship that's all about Him and not based on our knowledge of Him or our works.

> » *How has a lack of communication affected a relationship you've had or have? How has consistent communication affected a relationship?*

Today we will focus on Praising God and tomorrow on Repentance. On Thursday we study Asking for Others and Ourselves, then on Friday we move toward Yielding to God. Before we do that, let's first look at prayer as a whole. Your head likely knows and believes these things already. However, we want our hearts to be refreshed in hope through prayer.

> » *How would you describe your prayer life?*

» Do you feel confident or insecure with prayer? Why?

Let's look at what the Bible says about prayer.

Write what you learn about prayer from each of these verses:

- *Matthew 6:5*

- *Romans 12:12*

- *Ephesians 6:18*

- *Philippians 4:6*

- *Colossians 4:2*

- *1 Thessalonians 5:17*

At the time of writing this study, I was in the midst of a lot of unknowns.
» Are you in a season of unknown? How so?

A few months ago I went to my doctor because I felt off. My doc, knowing I'm the opposite of a hypochondriac, ran some tests just to see if anything was going on. The first round came back abnormal, so they ran another to double check things. That's when I got the call that has taken over our lives the past couple of months: "Mrs. Kiser, we are going to need to refer you to an oncologist. Your numbers went up from our last test." Shocked, all I could blurt out was, "I'm sorry, what?" She repeated, "Your numbers are just mildly elevated but enough that we need you to be seen by a specialist."

So many questions. So many fears. If I'm being honest, which I promise to be throughout this study, all I could pray was: "Please Lord, not cancer. Your will and way is best...I believe. Help my unbelief...Oh crap. Only Jesus..." I repeated those words again and again. I took refuge in the honest prayers uttered by King David (Psalms), Jesus in the Garden (Matthew 26), and the father wanting his son to be healed (Mark 9:24).

Finally, I sat before the oncologist as he looked over my most recent tests and said, "We will do further testing but it looks like it could be one of two things: a rare blood disorder that's easily treated or leukemia." Leukemia. It wasn't at all how I expected that first appointment to go. Again, I questioned the medical professionals as if they don't know what they are doing and my questions could change their assumptions: "I'm sorry, but you actually think I could have cancer?!" To which he flatly said, "Yes." He followed it up to say that some people test higher in all these areas and it's nothing, so it could be that too, but that is very rare.

More waiting. More repeating my prayer strain. Every moment of every day was clouded with this unknown. Every dance party with my three little girls, every date night with my husband, every time I sat to write this Lent study, every time I met with friends or worshiped at church. I believed Jesus could heal me. I actually believed He could take this away. I also knew, from the gospels, that sometimes He allows things to happen that we will never like or understand.

Finally the day came, and with my heart literally pounding out of my chest, I heard the doctor say, "Not cancer." But I'm still waiting in the unknown. I've been transferred to another specialist and now we just wait to see what is going on.

Unknowns are hard. The hardest part of the unknown is the darkness.

So many have asked me how I'm feeling now that I know it's not cancer. Truth? I'm struggling more today than I was before hearing "not cancer." The unknown is so much harder, for me at least, because it is so out of my control. I know leukemia would not have been awesome, so please don't hear that I'd prefer that. However, there was a comfort and unusual sense of control in having what's happening to me narrowed down. Now we are back in the unknown.

>> *How does the darkness of your unknown make you feel?*

>> *How does it affect how you follow Christ?*

>> **Read John 8:12 and write it out below:**

Our only way out of the darkness is Jesus. I don't say that as an easy Christian default answer, I say that because it's truth, my friend. Jesus never promised us a lack of unknown (or darkness). He simply promised us light in the darkness.

One of the things I love about Lent (and Advent), is we get to physically experience the light of Christ as we use candles (see the introduction for more information on Lenten candles).

Today we can praise God because He is light. Each day of this study we will start it by praising God—acknowledging who He is, what He's done, and what He will do! When we do this the unknowns of our lives don't feel as dark. When we focus on the Light, and less on our unknowns, our lives are filled with hope.

Spend the rest of today praising God in the following areas:

• *Ways He has worked in the Bible:*

• *Ways He has worked in your past:*

• *What you see today—His created things:*

• *For the people He has placed in your life:*

- *Healing (big or small):*

- *When He said no or did something you didn't like at the time:*

- *When He said yes or amazed you with what He did at the time:*

- *For your daily provisions:*

- *Anything else:*

WHAT SHOULD I DO?

How can you apply what you have heard today? (James 1:22)

_____

_____

_____

WHO SHOULD I TELL?

What is something you can share about today? Who should you share this with?

_____

_____

_____

SHARE WHAT GOD IS TEACHING YOU!

Justice through Repentance

PRAISE GOD. REPENT OF SINS.

_____

_____

_____

_____

Today is Ash Wednesday, the official first day of Lent. For some of you this day may have rich significance, for others of you this day may have always been like any other day.

Here's why it is a significant day for all of us who believe in Jesus, regardless of which denomination we align with: Ash Wednesday starts us off where we should start off more often—on our knees before God. Ash Wednesday is a day marked in ashes—shifting our focus to repentance. Ashes were historically a symbol of repentance and sorrow. In addition, ashes acknowledge what God said in Genesis 3:19, "For you are dust, and to dust you shall return."

Repentance isn't fun or easy, but it brings about real life. I love you too much to skip past what is best for all of us, so today we are going to do the dirty work of repentance.

» How would you define repentance?

I have three kids six and younger, so the words "I'm sorry" are said frequently in our house—by kids and adults! Something I have to say to my girls often is, "We can't just say we are sorry with our words, we need to say sorry with our actions." That is repentance—turning from the sin in your life to God. To simply say we are sorry isn't full repentance, but it is a great first step. Our actions prove we mean the words we say.

☐ **Use the following page to confess any sin in your life. These can be sins that have crept up today and also sins that seem to continuously pop up again and again. (Just fill out the first column, we will get to the second one after.)**

CONFESS	REPENT/TURN AWAY

☐ **Now go back to each of those things and ask God to show you how to turn away from those things. List out some of the turning back to God ideas that He gives you. Then ask Him to help you make these a reality. You might even want to take a picture of this part and send it to some of your most trusted friends.**

Here is the beautiful thing about combining repentance with justice today: we must humble ourselves to best serve others. 2 Corinthians 12:9 says, "He (Jesus) said to me, 'My grace is sufficient for you, for my power is made perfect in weakness.' Therefore, I will boast all the more gladly of my weaknesses, so that the power of Christ may rest upon me."

☐ **Go back to the previous page of sins listed out and smudge a big cross on top of it. Do this however you symbolically can, as if it were ashes actually smudged over your sin. As you smudge the cross on top of your sin, embrace His forgiveness for your life.**

WHAT SHOULD I DO?

How can you apply what you have heard today? (James 1:22)

_____

_____

WHO SHOULD I TELL?

What is something you can share about today? Who should you share this with?

_____

_____

SHARE WHAT GOD IS TEACHING YOU!

@sacredholidays   #sacredholidays

Ask for Others and Yourself

PRAISE GOD. REPENT OF SINS. ASK FOR OTHERS AND YOURSELF.

_____

_____

_____

_____

Asking is a part of our prayer life that most of us, even those who don't believe, feel most comfortable with. We don't mind praying for others or even ourselves and the beautiful thing is, our Father wants us to ask.

» *Write out Matthew 7:7-8, 11*

I'm a total word nerd. Not in the grammar sense because I don't even know the difference between a comma and a semicolon. Not even in the big word kind of a way, because who really talks like that? I love the meaning of words. I love that a single word can really mean 10 things. Definitions are so much fun for me. My college Sunday School teacher was super into studying Greek words, and it changed the way I studied the Bible. It was like finding a trap door leading to secret passages in a room you already loved.

The very first word I ever looked up was "ask" in Matthew 7:7. I love to use Zodhiates' Complete Word Study Dictionary alongside an Exhaustive Concordance, but you can also go to www.biblestudytools.com to look up word meanings for free! There, they define Ask:

"Aiteo: to ask, beg, call for, crave, desire, require."

Once I understood that asking God for others and for myself is nothing like sitting on Santa's lap, the way I prayed began to change.

Write your own definition for the words that define "ask":

• *Beg:*

• *Call for:*

• *Crave:*

• *Desire:*

• *Require:*

When we come to Him begging Him to_____,
calling for him to_____, craving that He would_____, desiring
that He would_____, and requiring that He would_____; it
changes everything. No longer are we muttering off our wish list, but we are bringing all
our hope to the Giver of all good things (James 1:17).
   » Read Luke 8:40-56 and write what you learn about asking God.

This story involves several people, but specifically two—a man with a dying 12-year-old
daughter and a woman who had been bleeding for 12 years.

   They exemplify the honest process of praying—we desire for God to work, we aren't
sure how to come to Him, we have faith, we lose faith, we feel like a burden, we choose to
be bold anyway, and so on. I hope you feel freedom to just come to Jesus. There isn't one
right way to ask.

   » Do you struggle to ask Jesus for things? Why or why not?

Your Father wants you to come to Him. He longs for you to come to Him.

   » What do you want to ask, beg, call for, crave, desire, or require of your Father today?

Obviously God's will and way will be done. We see that. Oftentimes that isn't the same as our way (Isaiah 55:8-9). We pray "your will be done," but we don't let that hinder our faith that He can do it. This woman had struggled with this sickness for 12 years. 12 years.

» *How old were you 12 years ago? What was your life like then?*

» *Is there something you have been praying for a long time?*

She hadn't lost hope yet. You know she had tried everything at this point. The kind of faith to believe that simply touching Jesus's garment would heal her is amazing, especially after 12 years of struggling through this. For 12 years she had longed for healing.

We know the story of her healing, so sometimes that is all we remember about her. What we forget is that for 12 years she didn't get her way, she didn't get the miracle; she got the waiting.

» *When God answers our prayers differently than we want, does it change His goodness?*

Then we have the father who didn't want to inconvenience Jesus once his daughter was declared dead. Hope was gone.

» *Do you feel hopeless about anything you've been praying about? How has this changed what you believe about your situation or the goodness of God?*

» *Write out Luke 8:54-55.*

Our God is able to do what seems impossible. His timing rarely matches up with our own. His goodness is for you. His power unlimited. He can do anything. Ask Him. Watch and see. He says in Matthew 17:20 that all we need is faith like a mustard seed and we can move mountains. Bring your faith to Him and ask.

WHAT SHOULD I DO?

How can you apply what you have heard today? (James 1:22)

_____

_____

WHO SHOULD I TELL?

What is something you can share about today? Who should you share this with?

_____

_____

SHARE WHAT GOD IS TEACHING YOU!

Yield to God

PRAISE GOD. REPENT OF SINS. ASK FOR OTHERS AND YOURSELF.

YIELD TO GOD.

_____

_____

_____

_____

Giving over control is hard. I'm a control freak, anyone else? This idea of yielding is one of my biggest struggles with the Lord. Yield is a fancy way to say give over. Our way of saying: "Everything I have is yours God. Use me for your glory."

» *How do you see yield to be different than asking?*

Asking involves a specific request or need, yielding is just surrender. I often use this time to go through what I have going on during the day and ask that God would use it for His glory, to move powerfully through me, to help me love those I'll encounter, and so on.

» *Read and write out Ephesians 5:1-2.*

This next step in our prayer model is yielding just as Christ yielded Himself, the story of Lent—Christ loved and gave Himself up for us. When we realize this, then we want to imitate Him, the greatest example of love there ever has been, the most beautiful offering to God. So we open up our hands and our plans to God, and we ask Him to conform them to His ways.

» *Read and write out Romans 12:1-2.*

Let's practice this right now!

» *List what you have planned today (or tomorrow if it is evening).*

Go through each item and give those to God. Ask Him to show you how to imitate Him as you _____. Ask Him to make _____ a fragrant offering. Ask Him to renew your mind as you _____.

It's good to do this with any future ideas or plans we have. As we hold the things in our lives loosely before Him we can walk more freely with Him.

» *Go through the same process for future plans. List out some upcoming things or dreams.*

» *What did Ephesians 5:1 call you to be?*

» *Have you ever played Simon Says? What's the key to winning?*

You've got to pay attention if you want to win. You can't look around. You have to pay attention and listen intently. It's similar to following Jesus—the more we listen directly to Him the more like Him we become.

» *Have you ever hung out with someone so much that you started to become more like them?*

I'm so excited for us this next seven weeks—we are going to basically stalk Jesus's final days. We are going to go slowly through His final weeks on earth because we don't want to miss a single lesson. As we look at Him we will be able imitate Him! I can't wait to see who we become over the next seven weeks!

WHAT SHOULD I DO?

How can you apply what you have heard today? (James 1:22)

_____

_____

_____

WHO SHOULD I TELL?

What is something you can share about today? Who should you share this with?

_____

_____

_____

SHARE WHAT GOD IS TEACHING YOU!

Sabbath

PRAISE GOD. REPENT OF SINS. ASK FOR OTHERS AND YOURSELF.

YIELD TO GOD. WAIT AND LISTEN.

Waiting, ugh. None of us like it. Not fun or easy. And silence and listening comes in as a close second. In our world of instant everything we are becoming weaker and weaker in the skill of waiting and listening.

However, the Bible is pretty clear that Sabbath, or resting and waiting and listening, is a pretty important discipline to God.

Read the following Scriptures and write out what they teach you about Sabbath, waiting, silence and listening:

- *Genesis 2:3*

- *Exodus 20:8-11*

- *Matthew 14:13*

- *Matthew 14:23*

- *Mark 1:35*

- *Mark 2:27*

- *Luke 5:15-16*

- *Luke 6:12*

We are going to practice this day once a week. For most of us (like me) who don't regularly practice actual resting, this will be really hard. There is also not one right way to do this, but there is a best way for you.

» **What is most restful (recharging) for you?**

» **How is that different from what you do when you're being lazy?**

» **What helps you hear from God best?**

Whatever you wrote down, make every effort to do those things on your Sabbath/Rest days.

weekly plan

WEEK DAY	✓	ITEM(S) TO DO	OBSTACLES	SOLUTIONS
SUN				
MON				
TUES				
WED				
THUR				
FRI				
SAT				

FASTING

This week I will fast from:

_____

I am fasting from this because:

_____

In order to keep this fast, I need to:

_____

Week 2

Walk in the Light (Blow Out First Candle)

Faith & Fruit

Get Angry & Make Space

Sons & Tenants

Prayer through Song

Sabbath

Walk in the Light

PRAISE GOD. REPENT OF SINS. ASK FOR OTHERS AND YOURSELF.

YIELD TO GOD. WAIT AND LISTEN.

This is a big day because up until this point, Jesus would instruct people not to tell what He had done or who He was. Today He calls Himself "Lord."

> » *Read Matthew 21:1-11 and record below all the things that happened.*
> *(If you have extra time, you can also read Mark 11, Luke 19, and John 12:12.)*

The beauty of this moment is the Savior of the world, your Savior, didn't come in on a private jet with an entourage of bodyguards and decked out SUVs. Your Savior came on the back of a donkey.

> » *What does Jesus coming on a donkey mean to you? What does it say about Him?*

> » *Imagine the crowds of people before Jesus came (this is hypothetical, of course, but let's just imagine). Who were they? What did they do during the day? What were their struggles? What were their joys?*

» Read Matthew 21:9 and write out what the crowds shouted.

Commentaries vary on the exact contextual translation for this phrase. In years past it would've meant, "God save us." In future years, it was an exclamation that God has saved them! Either way, we get a glimpse into the people and what they were longing for—God's salvation!

» Do you feel like you need God to save or rescue you? List out some ways below. (God continues to rescue us even after we believe in Him. His rescuing isn't just once at salvation.)

The more we recognize our need for a Savior the better off we are. We can't do this on our own; we weren't meant to.

(YOU SHOULD HAVE 6 LIT)

Jesus came into our brokenness, our sin, and our not enough-ness (I might make up words sometimes, consider yourself warned) on the back of a donkey, and He answered the cries for a Savior.

» Read 1 John 1:5-9 and note Jesus's and our relationship with light.

As we blow out our first candle this week, it is a reminder that on our own we are without light, on our own we can't do it. We need Jesus. We need Him to save us. We need His light in our lives. He came to cleanse us and bring light into our lives. He came to save so we didn't have to save ourselves, knowing we never could.

WHAT SHOULD I DO?

How can you apply what you have heard today? (James 1:22)

_____

_____

_____

WHO SHOULD I TELL?

What is something you can share about today? Who should you share this with?

_____

_____

_____

SHARE WHAT GOD IS TEACHING YOU!

Faith and Fruit

PRAISE GOD. REPENT OF SINS. ASK FOR OTHERS AND YOURSELF.

YIELD TO GOD. WAIT AND LISTEN.

We start our journey today of Jesus's final days. You are going to fall in love with the humanity of Jesus today as we get to see how He was fully man and, in the same moment, fully God.

> » *Read Matt 21:18-22 and record what happens.*
> *(You can also read Mark 11:12-14, 20-26 for another gospel perspective.)*

» **What shows He is fully man?**

» **What shows He is fully God?**

I think Jesus might have been a little hangry here (hungry + angry). We've all been there, right? We are so hungry we might be a little unreasonable. I can't go so far to say Jesus was being unreasonable, because He is Jesus, but maybe a little.

Here's the deal, while the Scripture tells us it wasn't the season for figs, He wasn't being completely ridiculous to expect to find fruit. Once fig trees start to grow leaves, the fruit grows quickly afterwards. So since there were already leaves, it wasn't too far fetched to think there would also be figs.

There is a parallel to our lives here. Often times we can do all the things to give the appearance of growth and life. We go to church, Bible study, don't say certain things or watch other things; we are modest in appearance and simple in life, etc. Yet the Word of God doesn't dwell in us (or us in it) and we don't aim to love God and others with all that we are. We don't live surrendered to Him. Other than our right actions and choices, there's little actual fruit in our lives.

Mark where you are, then share why you marked that.

Withered	Leaves Sprouting	Fruitful

» Why did you mark yourself where you did?

Jesus cursed the tree and it withered immediately! Jesus doesn't mess around. In our tolerance-centered culture, we forget about the justice of God. We forget that He didn't care about relevance, like we do. We are made righteous through Him, not through our own efforts.

» How did Peter respond when He saw the tree had actually withered? Would you have responded the same way? (Mark 11:21)

God's judgment can often be surprising. Didn't He come to save? Wasn't He supposed to bring peace? We learn in this story that the Lord has no interest in tolerating our facades. He couldn't care less if we come across like we have it all together. He wants us to be submitted to Him and bearing His fruit because He lives within us.

» Read Galatians 5:16-24. Write out the fruit:

In college I remember reading about the fruit of the Spirit and writing out each word on a notecard and putting it on my wall. I would pray that the Lord would gift me with each of these. I would work hard to have more patience, be kinder, exhibit more self-control, etc. I had it all wrong, even though my intentions were pure. I was trying to grow my own fruit. My efforts or intentions weren't bad, but they were just leaves.

» What is necessary for fruit to grow in you? (Gal 5:16, 22)

The only answer is the Spirit. And we don't really know what to do with the Spirit, but we need to know so we can stop our efforts to grow fruit and instead let the Spirit grow it within us.

Read these verses on the Spirit. Write what you learn about Him:
  • *John 14:26-27*

  • *Romans 8:26-28*

What a kind Savior, He doesn't leave us to ourselves to figure this out. If He did, all we would be able to produce are leaves. Instead, He sent a Helper! This is actually the story of Lent: He doesn't leave us, He makes sure we are more than taken care of.

» What does having faith and moving mountains have to do with a cursed fig tree? Does this seem strange to you? (Mark 11:22-24)

Nothing is impossible for those who believe. Nothing. Even that thing that keeps you from bearing fruit (temptations or sin), even that thing can be moved!

» What keeps you from bearing fruit?

Even those things cannot keep you from Him. If He can move mountains then He can remove whatever you wrote above. His Word says it can happen if we do not doubt in our hearts and believe that it will come to pass (Mark 11:23). The issue has never been God's ability, it's been our doubting and lack of belief that keeps many of His miracles from happening.

Finally, He gives us one final part to the equation to see miracles.

» What do we need to do before we pray? (Mark 11:25)

Forgiveness is so hard. It's something we often sweep over all past hurts. We don't want to stir things up; we don't want to go through it all again. We have confused stuffing our emotions down for forgiveness. Ignoring things that have hurt you isn't forgiveness. Avoiding drama and confrontation isn't forgiveness. Forgiveness is hard but it is also healing. Forgiveness doesn't always make things better, but it makes your heart better.

» How do you define forgiveness? If you aren't sure, do a word study on forgiveness.

» Is there anyone you need to forgive today?

WHAT SHOULD I DO?

How can you apply what you have heard today? (James 1:22)

_____

_____

WHO SHOULD I TELL?

What is something you can share about today? Who should you share this with?

_____

_____

SHARE WHAT GOD IS TEACHING YOU!

@sacredholidays   #sacredholidays

Get Angry and Make Space

PRAISE GOD. REPENT OF SINS. ASK FOR OTHERS AND YOURSELF.

YIELD TO GOD. WAIT AND LISTEN.

_____

_____

_____

_____

_____

We are about to read a story about Jesus that, had we not already heard before, would be very shocking. The actions He exhibits are so unlike the guy we think had come to bring peace to the world.

» Read Matthew 21:12-17 and note what happens below.

(You can read the same account in Mark 11:15-19 and Luke 19:45-48. There is an earlier account of temple clearing in John 2:13-22, but this is considered a different temple clearing taking place earlier in His ministry.)

» Why did Jesus react the way He did?

» Do you think Jesus was angry? If yes, was it OK to be angry? If not, what was He then? Were these emotions justified or holy?

Anger is an uncomfortable and uncertain emotion, one we don't really know what to do with. We all feel it. Right? We just don't know what to do with it. For most of us, our anger issues are rooted more in selfishness than in justice.

Earlier I asked you if Jesus was angry when He kicked people out of the House of God and flipped over the tables of people selling things. For years I've always said that there is no way He was angry because I didn't believe Jesus could be angry, He was being just. Which is true in a small part. As I get older and my worldview expands past my own circumstances, I believe now that there are two types of anger—justice-based anger and self-based anger. I believe Jesus was showing us what justice based anger looks like.

» *Read Ephesians 4:26-27 and write what you learn about anger.*

Anger is allowed when it isn't rooted in sin. It is possible to be angry and yet not sin.

» *Do you believe that is possible? Have you ever experienced this personally or witnessed it in another?*

Next I'm going to ask you to make a chart to help you identify what is justice-based anger and what is self-based anger. Before I ask you to do that, I thought I'd share a few personal examples to get you started.

Justice-Based Anger: Anything that causes displeasure to the heart of God.

This anger wouldn't bring about any form of sin in your heart or actions. Personal Examples: Hearing that there are 27 million slaves in our world today, this makes me livid. Knowing that right this minute there are thousands of children in our city that are in the foster system without a mom or dad loving them well, and thousands more that should be because their home life is so abusive and neglectful. Knowing that there are many churches and ministries that care more about profits and bottom lines and popularity, but their leaders' hearts are far from God.

Self-Based Anger: Anything that displeases you and leads to sin of any kind.

When my girls don't listen for the one millionth time that day (which often leads to me overreacting in some way). When Chris asks me what budget category my recent Target splurge will come out of (which generally leads to be making some disrespectful response). When I hear about someone else's success (and it leads me to being envious and wishing they weren't as successful). When I am left out (and it leads me to self wallow and pulling away from community).

Take some time and list out your own examples:

JUSTICE-BASED ANGER	*SELF-BASED ANGER*

Our society is ill-equipped for dealing with anger and so we handle it poorly.

Justice-based anger is allowed. In fact there are some things we need to get angry about! I know this will feel so wrong for most of us, but as long as it doesn't turn into sin it is just anger. Sometimes we need to flip over some tables. Sometimes we've been sitting still, trying not to be angry, when it's time to flip some tables over. When we take our eyes off the things that make us angry due to our selfish desires, then we can get angry about the things that shame the heart of God. Then we can get up and stop the whining and start flipping some things over.

» *Are there any tables you need to flip?*

» *What did Jesus say we've made His house? (v13)*

» *What did He say His house should be? (v13)*

Jesus wants us to keep what is holy, holy. Sometimes to keep things holy we need to flip somethings upside down. Oh, this is so hard for me. To look at my own life and think what needs to be flipped upside down and thrown out so I can be a House of Prayer, sounds like a scary activity. Sounds like something that won't be easy, that will require change.

» *Re-read verse 14 and write it out below. Circle who Jesus helped and underline what He did.*

When we clear out what isn't necessary, it creates space for what is best. When Jesus cleared out the tables for those who were selling things, it created space for healing.

Let's create space today so healing can come—for us and others!

WHAT SHOULD I DO?

How can you apply what you have heard today? (James 1:22)

WHO SHOULD I TELL?

What is something you can share about today? Who should you share this with?

SHARE WHAT GOD IS TEACHING YOU!

Sons and Tenants

PRAISE GOD. REPENT OF SINS. ASK FOR OTHERS AND YOURSELF.

YIELD TO GOD. WAIT AND LISTEN.

Jesus loved to tell stories. Do you know anyone like that—they have a story for everything? Jesus's stories, or parables, can be a little confusing to understand. This is because their contexts are different than our personal context today, and it seems Jesus intended for them to be a little confusing (Matthew 13:13).

One of the things I love about His stories is they force me to slow down and think through them. Some meanings are obvious and some really take re-reading the text multiple times, thinking about it, reading commentaries, etc., before it comes to light.

Today we are going to read two parables. I'm not going to write very much commentary in between because I want you to do the work of figuring out what it means. You can do this. Don't skip parts. Give it time. Let the Helper, the Holy Spirit, show you the meaning of Jesus's words. Listen.

Before we read these two parables, it's important to know who is talking, who He is talking to, and where He is saying these things.

Read Matthew 21:23 and fill in the answers below:

» Who was talking?

» Where was He talking?

» *Who were they talking to?*

» *What was Jesus doing when they approached Him?*

» *Read Matthew 21:28-32 and summarize what occurred below:*

» *Had you heard Jesus's story for the first time that day, how would you have answered His questions in v31?*

This can be a confusing story. Let's put ourselves in the disciples' shoes and see what we can undertand about what Jesus was saying.

» *Which son do you relate to most? How so? If neither, write out a description for a third son that you'd relate to.*

» *What do you think Jesus was trying to teach from this parable? How could you apply that lesson?*

Our words are not enough. Saying the right Christian answers without the actions to back them up is actually fruitless.

» *Read James 2:14-17 and write out verse 17 below:*

Works without faith is legalism and faith without works is dead, meaning it is nothing. The magic, really the holiness and power, in our following Jesus happens when faith and works collide. When we stop saying the right things and thinking the right things, but our actions prove our beliefs. It should not be confusing what your are about, your faith should be made indisputable by your works.

» Now read the next parable in Matthew 21:33-46 and summarize what happens:
(You can read other occurrences of this parable in Mark 12:1-12 and Luke 20:9-18.)

» Who had done all the work at the vineyard? Who does this character represent? (v33)

» Who occupied the vineyard? What does their title indicate about their right to the harvest? Who does this group of people represent? (v33)

» What was the master's expectation? (v34)

» Why did the tenants respond the way they did? (v35-39)

» What do you think Jesus was trying to teach from this parable?

WHAT SHOULD I DO?

How can you apply what you have heard today? (James 1:22)

WHO SHOULD I TELL?

What is something you can share about today? Who should you share this with?

SHARE WHAT GOD IS TEACHING YOU!

Prayer through Song

PRAISE GOD. REPENT OF SINS. ASK FOR OTHERS AND YOURSELF. YIELD TO GOD. WAIT AND LISTEN.

_____

_____

_____

_____

_____

I hope this study shows you different ways to connect with God outside of the focused, sit-down time you have with Him. As much as we need to make studying His Word a priority and a diligent practice, we also need to be women who walk with Him all the time. We need to be able to walk with Him shame free on the days we don't have a "quiet time" or whatever else you call your time with the Lord.

> **» Do you struggle with walking with God outside of your time with Him?**

Prayer is a big part of connecting with God throughout the day. There are countless verses on why we should pray and how we should pray in the Bible. Google "verses on prayer" and you can read for hours on why and how to pray.

Here's the truth: there isn't a magical formula to praying. Praying is just talking to God. In fact our prayer lives will be more genuine the less impressive they are. He doesn't care about your fancy words or passionate speech. He wants you to talk to Him and listen to His response, and then go back and forth again and again.

It's one of the best gifts He has given us that we get to talk with Him.

I've found several ways that are helpful for me when I talk to God (prayer). I'm going to walk you through a few of those ways over the next six weeks on these prayer days. Remember all of these are just suggestions. They are NOT more "shoulds" to add to your Christian checklist. They are just ideas from a fellow sister. Feel free to do these suggestions or try something outside your normal prayer routine to talk with God.

Today's prayer activity is listening to music.

So easy, right? I would suggest aiming to do two things today:

1. **First, listen to worship music all alone and worship without hindrance.**

Some of us worship freely at church or at retreats, but have never had a similar experience in our own homes. Today is the day.

Two things to nail down: song choice and location.

Song choice: If you have a favorite worship album, play that. Or maybe choose a Pandora station or Spotify list. If you need suggestions, my personal favorite worship leaders are: Hillsong, All Sons & Daughters, Shane & Shane, Christy Nockels, Bethel, Kari Jobe, and Lauren Daigle.

Location: Where can you go to be totally private or free? For some of you this is easy, for others you will have to be creative. Maybe it's after everyone in your home is asleep or before they wake up. Maybe you need to go to your car. I'm not sure what works for you, but don't let your current setup be an excuse to not do it.

> *» Where did you go? How did it work? What could you do differently next time to make the time work better?*

> *» How did this time worshiping affect your heart for God?*

2. **Second, listen to worship music and only worship music for the whole day. (Yep, no TV or other songs.)**

I'm not a Christian Music Only/Nothing Secular person. However, I do believe there is a great benefit to exposing our ears to only things that specifically connect our hearts to God for a period of time. Today, turn off whatever noise you usually have going and just play worship music. Then take notice of how it affects you throughout the day.

> *» How did it go listening to worship music all day?*

> *» Do you feel like God spoke anything to you during this time?*

> *» Did it change how you lived and loved?*

Sabbath

PRAISE GOD. REPENT OF SINS. ASK FOR OTHERS AND YOURSELF.

YIELD TO GOD. WAIT AND LISTEN.

Today might feel awkward. It might even feel forced. Remember what we said last week, practicing Sabbath isn't something most of us are familiar with. Most of us have all tried a new eating or work out plan; I mean "life style change" (please tell me you are laughing at yourself for past attempts at this). What we can learn from this is changing anything will never feel natural at first. We can also learn that it doesn't necessarily get easier and temptations don't go away just because we become more comfortable in the practice of it.

We must commit and block off our Sabbath to make it happen.

This isn't a day we will guide you through. It's a day just for you and Him, a day of rest (which isn't the same thing as a day of laziness).

» What brings you rest that you will do today?

» How will you protect your Sabbath and keep it Holy (Exodus 20:8)?

Come back and journal here about your day before you go to sleep.

» *What did you learn about God on your Sabbath?*

» *What did you learn about yourself?*

» *What do you need to do or not do next time to make for a more holy Sabbath?*

» *Anything else you learned or realized or noticed today?*

weekly plan

WEEK DAY	✓	ITEM(S) TO DO	OBSTACLES	SOLUTIONS
SUN				
MON				
TUES				
WED				
THUR				
FRI				
SAT				

FASTING

This week I will fast from:

_____

I am fasting from this because:

_____

In order to keep this fast, I need to:

_____

Week 3

No Fear in the Light (Blow Out Second Candle)

Our Heart with Money

Poured Out & Hair Down

7 Woes

Prayer through Silence

Sabbath

No Fear in the Light

PRAISE GOD. REPENT OF SINS. ASK FOR OTHERS AND YOURSELF.

YIELD TO GOD. WAIT AND LISTEN.

Fears can be crippling or at best limiting. Fears have kept me from so many good things. Fear of failure kept me from writing for years. Fear of success kept me from starting a business. (Only us women could have a fear of failure and success at the same time. Ha!) Fear of rejection has kept me from so many amazing friendships. Fear of quitting again has kept me from so many healthy choices. Fear of loneliness had me in countless wrong relationships, both dating and friendships. I could fill all the pages of this study with my fears.

» *What are some fears you have? What do they keep you from?*

» *Read Psalm 27:1 and write out what three things are said of the Lord:*

Have you ever tried to go to the bathroom in the middle of the night? Or been walking to your front door once it's already dark out? It's hard to do! Before cell phones, I'm not sure what people did. That built-in flashlight has done amazing things for helping us see in the dark. It's crazy what such a small light can do to fill an entire room.

BLOW OUT ONE CANDLE

(YOU SHOULD HAVE 5 LIT)

» *How do your fears and darkness feel similar?*

The unknown is the worst. Not being sure what will happen can cripple us.

Let's define the three descriptors of God from Psalm 27:1. Don't stress over this, there isn't a right or wrong answer. Just write what He means to you in each of these contexts.

» *My Light:*

» *My Salvation:*

» Stronghold of my life:

When we focus less on what we fear and focus more on God, then the fears lessen. I love how The Message translates this verse: "Light, space, zest—that's God! So, with him on my side I'm fearless, afraid of no one and nothing." All of a sudden what we fear, our worst-case scenarios, aren't as scary. The unknown remains unknown, but our Light, our Salvation, our Stronghold is with us.

I met a woman this past year whose story I will never forget. She had experienced so much loss—a stillborn, a miscarriage, and then lost two babies during their first years of life. Just a few years following those tragedies, she found out her husband wanted out of their marriage and had already been involved with others. I'm not sure I've heard a more devastating story. I don't know how you recover from that.

One night, a group of us gathered around a fireplace with tears streaming down all of our cheeks as she continued her story, "You know what? People tell me, 'That's the worst story imaginable. Nothing is more horrible than what you've been through.' For years I agreed. For years I believed that to be true. But you know what? It isn't the worst. The worst would be to be without Jesus."

I was speechless. I couldn't imagine saying the same thing.

Remember how I had shared the story about my cancer scare this past fall? That first call telling me I needed to see an oncologist came days before I left for this retreat to meet this woman. Her perspective shifted how I walked through this health scare the following months. When things would become scary or dark, I'd remember, "The worst would be to be without Jesus." So He became everything for me. When I'd fear what would happen to my girls if they lost their mom or if Chris would still think I was beautiful if I lost my hair, I'd remember that Jesus was the only thing I needed.

Let's apply this principle to our fears we listed out. Write out your fears on the left. Then draw an arrow, connecting each fear to "God is Light."

FEAR OR UNKNOWN	GOD IS LIGHT

I know it's scary. I don't ever mean to say that our struggles aren't struggles. Your struggles aren't insignificant. There's a reason the Bible says "Do not fear," or some variation of that more than 300 times. He sees your fear and doesn't want you to be fearful any longer.

» Write this down: He sees my fear.

He isn't telling you to get over it. He is telling you to let Him into it.

» Read Psalm 56:8-13 and note what it means to you.

You have a good Father who takes note of all your emotions. He tenderly saves them and treasures them. Not a one is wasted on Him. He will deliver you. While things seem dark, light is coming when we trust in Him.

WHAT SHOULD I DO?

How can you apply what you have heard today? (James 1:22)

WHO SHOULD I TELL?

What is something you can share about today? Who should you share this with?

SHARE WHAT GOD IS TEACHING YOU!

Our Heart with Money

PRAISE GOD. REPENT OF SINS. ASK FOR OTHERS AND YOURSELF.

YIELD TO GOD. WAIT AND LISTEN.

_____

_____

_____

_____

_____

I love these Scripture days when we simply focus on His Word. I'm excited about this study for you, for all of us, for so many reasons. One of the main reasons is that I hope that at the end of it you have greater confidence in studying His Word and walking with Him in new ways. There isn't one way to follow Him. There isn't one way to spend time with God. There isn't one way to study His Word. There isn't one way to pray. All we know is that He does want us to do each of these things. So we make our offerings to Him with our time and affections.

Today we are going to look at offerings in a different context—financial. Ugh. I know. Maybe for some of you this isn't a hard one. Maybe finances aren't a stress for you, and that's awesome! Even so, stay open to what the Spirit wants to teach you. Today's parables are for all of us—whether destitute or rich or something in between.

» **What are your feelings towards your finances today?**

» **Do you have debt? How much? Does this stress you?**

» Do you live outside your means (monthly income is less than what you spend)?

» Do you tithe? How much?

» Do you give outside of your tithe? How much?

» Where does the majority of your money go, not including necessary bills?

» Any other feelings or expressions in regards to your money?

Look over all those thoughts and take a moment and give them all to Jesus. Ask Him to bring healing to any wrong context, thoughts, feelings, and actions you've had with money. Ask Him to bring correction and hope and freedom. He gives it, friend. Always and abundantly.

I promise today won't be miserable. I can't promise today will feel awesome though. For most of us it might feel more like the first workout after a long season of inactivity. We might be sore, but it will be sore in a good, making progress kind of a way!

» Read the first Scripture for today in Mark 12:13-17 and summarize below:

(You can read other accounts of this parable in Matthew 22:15-22; Luke 20:19-26;)

(There's an entire study that could be made discussing the ways the Pharisees would try to trap Jesus. I'm going to skip past that today so we can focus more on finances. However, if you feel the Spirit convicting you or urging you to dig into this concept of trapping Jesus and think you need to focus on that instead, feel free!)

Summarize Jesus's stance on finances by finishing the following: (v17)

» *Give to Ceasar (the government) what is* _____.

» *Give to God the things that are* _____.

» *How did Jesus deduce or prove this formula? (v15-16)*

It wasn't even a complicated thing. The coin had the government's identification on it. The people lived under the rule of that government. The government required taxes to be paid. Pretty simple. Pay those you owe money too—your government or anyone else that is entitled to have what is yours.

I feel in our desire to "be good stewards," we've become really greedy. Most of us are consumed by it, even if we don't realize it. On the flip side, some of us just don't care. We care more about adventure and making a difference, even if we can't pay for it. We are swiping our cards in "acts of faith" and piling up the debt to do "what God has called us to do."

Where do you tend to fall?

Greedy _____ **Frivolous**

» *Why did you mark the way you did?*

Let's look at one more story of someone far more generous than most of us have ever dared to be. Then we will wrap up with some action steps. Hang with me and know that I love you. I am right there in the middle of this with you, in no way do I claim to have this beast of finances figured out yet. Let's stay open to what He wants to teach us.

» **Read our final parable for today in Mark 12:41-44 and make notes below:**

(You can read another account of this parable in Luke 21:1-4.)

» How were the two offerings different?

Our heart is everything. Giving out of obligation or because the Word encourages is good and expected. Jesus didn't rebuke those who were giving out of their abundance.

» Write out verse 44.

They gave from their excess, she gave all she had. Woah.

» What is "everything you have"? List out your assets (You don't have to put specific numbers, just list out the things you have that are of value and list out some number that would signify what's in the bank.)

» If Jesus said to give that all up today, would you?

I got sucked into The Crown on Netflix recently and finished up season one in a ridiculous amount of time, thanks to getting sick for a couple of days. I hope I'm not ruining the show for anyone since you can find out the details on the internet easily (spoiler alert if you keep reading this paragraph). Princess Margaret swore she would choose love over title and wealth if the Queen forced her to. However, at the end of it all, she chose the title and the wealth. I'm sure a lot more went into that choice, but it was prominent in her conversations with the Queen.

I know other people who have made similar sacrifices—choosing comfort over calling. The lure of the money is so enticing that it can convince us there is no other option.

» List out what you give your finances to:

» List out what you give your time to:

» Do either of these things show that you are giving out of abundance to God (meaning just giving Him your overflow), or does it show that He has everything you have to give?

» What are three practical steps you could take today to become more generous financially? Then write next to each thing how you can make that happen.

You did it! I hope we don't have to talk about money again during this study. I know it's a tender topic. But I love you too much to skip over it. Thanks for doing the hard work today to surrender your finances to the Lord. Thankfully tomorrow is a Sabbath day! We can use some good rest after that.

WHAT SHOULD I DO?

How can you apply what you have heard today? (James 1:22)

WHO SHOULD I TELL?

What is something you can share about today? Who should you share this with?

SHARE WHAT GOD IS TEACHING YOU!

Poured Out and Hair Down

PRAISE GOD. REPENT OF SINS. ASK FOR OTHERS AND YOURSELF.

YIELD TO GOD. WAIT AND LISTEN.

I love the gospels and how they give us different perspectives on the life of Jesus. Faith increases when we hear the same account of Jesus, seen from a slightly different angle. What a gift that He has given us to allow us insight into so many intimate parts of His life. Few moments in Scripture are as intimate as this one between Him and Mary as she anoints His feet.

There are a few accounts of Jesus's anointing in Scripture, and it can be confusing to know whether or not they overlap. Most of the details are the same, but each book offers a few additional details. Most commentaries agree that these three accounts are all in fact referring to the same moment.

I'm going to ask you to do a little extra reading today because I don't want you to miss any details, so we are going to read all three accounts that are given to us. It will be worth it, I promise. Take note of everything—the setting, the people, the sacrifice, the responses, etc.

» Read John 12:1-8 and note what happens below.

» Read Matthew 26:6-13 and note any additional information below.

Read Mark 14:3-9 and note any additional information below.

Turn back to the account in John 12. We are going to focus in on some of the details listed here. *So many places we could dive into—Lord show us where to focus. Lead us to what we need most.*

> **» How much did Judas want to sell the ointment for? What did he want to do with it instead?**

This is a hard one for me, and I feel certain I would've asked this same question long before Judas did. Actually, being a woman, I probably would've seen what Mary was up to and pulled her aside and advised her to do something else, anything else. Judas's exclamation that it's worth 300 denarii falls flat on our ears, all shock value gone. However, to know that one-day's wage was one denarii on average, changes the whole thing, doesn't it? That ointment was worth 10 months of work! Can you even imagine? If I found out Chris gave away 10 months of his salary I would freak out on him. But she didn't just give it away, she poured it out. Gone. Nothing to show for it.

I'm going to go somewhere, and I hope you stick with me. I don't think it's too far a stretch.

> **» Are you in a season of waiting right now? Or a season where you see very little significance? If not, then share about the most reason season of insignificance.**

This past year was my first year to really turn a profit (get paid beyond what my costs were) in any of my efforts with ministry—writing, speaking, etc. My pride has struggled with this so much. I've felt guilty that I wasn't contributing (which wasn't at all put on me by anyone but myself). I've felt guilty for spending savings so that I could write and print studies. Or pay for sitters with the entire amount I was paid to speak some place. I've had so many people give me that look after they hear what I do. You know the one that says they think I'm an idiot and should get a real job with a real paycheck or just embrace being a stay-at-home mom. Many have said or inferred that this work I have done the past seven years has been a waste. If I had kept working we could be in an even better situation financially. If I had chosen to be fully dedicated to my kiddos, then they'd be better behaved or I'd be more bonded to them (the later of which is ridiculous). All that I've poured out for seven years has seemed like a waste to most people, and on my weakest, most insecure days, I've agreed.

> **» Do you feel like this season is a waste? Or a past season that has seemed insignificant, do you count it as a waste?**

I love how brave Mary is here, she just didn't care. She loved Jesus and gave her very best for Him. Nothing is wasted.

I think back on these past seven years now and I don't see them as a waste any longer. I wanted so badly for things to go faster. I wanted so badly for those around me to be impressed. I wanted to contribute. I wanted to know I wasn't making a mistake, that there was meaning and purpose in what I was doing and what I was offering. That's what my flesh wanted. But my heart won out most days—more than anything I wanted Jesus, I wanted to say yes to Him in each of these moments. Very few people have these big breakthrough moments. It's a lot of little insignificant moments that create the significant.

» What did she wipe, and what did she use to wipe? (v3)

Mary is such a rule breaker. She went straight against cultural norms simply to honor Christ. There is nothing politically correct about this lady, and I love that about her. She isn't trying to do what's right or fit in, she is trying to do what tells God she loves Him the most and brings Him the most honor, even if she appears like a fool.

She wiped His feet. This is gross on so many accounts because in those days men wore sandals and walked on dirt roads. I feel certain that the fully man side of Christ probably had stinky feet that day. Servants were usually provided to wash the feet of guests. Servants. The lowest in the household would fall to their knees and scrub the dirt off the feet of strangers. Instead Mary fell to her knees and wiped the feet of the one she cared most about.

She used her hair. This is wild more than it is weird. Women kept their hair up, only unraveling it for their husbands. For Mary to unravel her hair for Jesus was one of the most intimate acts a woman could offer.

I don't want us to miss this, so I am going to ask you to give a little more time today. *If possible grab this book and get on your knees. (If it's not possible, stay right where you are.) Ask God the following questions and jot down any thoughts you have:*

» Is my current season insignificant? How so?

» What could I give you that is of value? (Think beyond finances.)

» Do I care too much about what others think of my plans?

» How could I humble myself more (bow and wash feet, a servant's job)?

» How could I be more brave (let hair down)?

I hope your time with your Father was sweet. I hope He spoke hope over you. I hope you keep asking these questions. You are brave. Actually you aren't. I don't know why our current Christian mantra is that we are brave, wild women. We aren't. On our own, apart from Christ, we just aren't really that brave. Usually our bravery apart from Christ is selfishness or foolishness.

He makes you brave. He makes you enough and able to do whatever it is He whispered to you today. Trust Him.

Mary's act of humility and courage for her King is considered His anointing for burial. She prepared His flesh to make the greatest sacrifice that gives us courage and new life!

I wonder what your courage and humility could do in Jesus's name. Go do it, friend!

WHAT SHOULD I DO?

How can you apply what you have heard today? (James 1:22)

_____

_____

_____

WHO SHOULD I TELL?

What is something you can share about today? Who should you share this with?

_____

_____

_____

7 Woes

PRAISE GOD. REPENT OF SINS. ASK FOR OTHERS AND YOURSELF.

YIELD TO GOD. WAIT AND LISTEN.

It's interesting that most of us are more concerned with how those who don't claim to follow Jesus are behaving more than we are concerned with how those who claim to follow Him act. We give ourselves the grace we've accepted and put all the rules and regulations on everyone else.

 » *Circle who Jesus rebuked more—sinners or the religious?*

I could be off, but from what I've read in Scripture, Jesus called out the religious frequently. He did address sin with sinners but he always did so privately and in a manner that showed them the grace and freedom offered in Him. They didn't always accept it, but they were never shamed into repentance.

How do you feel you come across to those who aren't Christians:

- *In your family:*

- *At work:*

- *Out in public:*

- *On social media:*

» *Read Matthew 23:1-12 and note what Jesus said about the scribes and Pharisees:*

I think our first reaction would be that we aren't the same. Our heads genuinely believe that we don't want the high places of honor or that we are busy with our words. We would never be like that. However, we need to press harder and really test our own hearts, actions, and motives.

» *Do you feel slighted when looked over for places of honor? This could include leadership at church, credit when you've done something, not being asked to be in a women's group or a service team, etc.*

Our social media world makes it harder and harder to not want to be seen. We feel the sting when others are praised and we, yet again, have been left out. We feel the burn when others are doing amazing things and we are stuck behind a desk all day or a pile of dishes that never decrease. We wouldn't ever want to be out in front but it still stings when we aren't chosen. Or the flip side, does it go to our head when we are part of the chosen few?

» *Read Matthew 23:13-36 and summarize each of the Seven Woes in the left column in the following chart:*

WOE	DEFINITION	RE-FINE

» *Now go back and define or elaborate and explain what each rebuke meant.*

» *Now, and this might take some time, re-write a comparable rebuke for yourself.*

» *Ask God to convict you and show you, even though this might feel uncomfortable.*

As our society, even our Christian culture, becomes more tolerant, we will struggle more and more with rebuke and correction. However, sometimes it's the very thing we need. Let today be a correcting day!

That was a lot of work, but I hope it was helpful and gave you some insight for yourself and also how you are with others.

» *Is there anyone you need to ask forgiveness? Go and do that.*

Here's the beauty of Lent, our Father knew we would mess things up royally. He knew we would make a mess of things. Left to our own resources that's exactly what we do. It's not just you. You aren't alone. You aren't the only one struggling with this concept. Our lack of doing things well is simply our proof that we desperately need a Savior.

When Jesus spoke these words to these people they had to carry the weight of their sin, we don't. We don't have to wait until Easter morning to be reminded that He came, He died, and He rose again. Those things brought up life again. Believing in Him and trusting in Him washes all of our muck away. We get to try again (and mess up again).

As I tell my girls daily, there is nothing you could do that could make Mommy stop loving you. I love you even more today than I did yesterday. It's interesting because I actually feel the meaning of those words more on the days their behavior is insane than I do on the days it's delightful. Nearly each time a lump forms in my throat as I remember Matthew 7:11, *"If you then, who are evil, know how to give good gifts to your children, how much more will your Father who is in heaven give good things to those who ask Him!"*

» *Wrap up today by writing "how much more" on something where you will see it today. Each time you see it, let it remind you that God loves you even more.*

WHAT SHOULD I DO?

How can you apply what you have heard today? (James 1:22)

WHO SHOULD I TELL?

What is something you can share about today? Who should you share this with?

SHARE WHAT GOD IS TEACHING YOU!

Prayer through Silence

PRAISE GOD. REPENT OF SINS. ASK FOR OTHERS AND YOURSELF.

YIELD TO GOD. WAIT AND LISTEN.

_____

_____

_____

_____

This is different than our Sabbath day. On our Sabbath we rest, today we are totally still—in action and word.

» Do you struggle to be still and silent?

It's funny because I can get frustrated with my kids for the constant noise in our house, yet I struggle to be silent.

It's never quiet in our home. Never. Chris and I will often look at each other and yell across the table: "ONE OF THESE DAYS WE WILL MISS THIS." And we both laugh. We've heard from enough empty nesters to know that we will miss our noisy home, even if we won't miss the fussing or fighting noises. If it's not the kiddos, it's the other things I fill the quiet spaces with—Netflix binging, podcasts, music (even Christian), work, friends, etc. All good things, but they become unhealthy when they occupy all my space, and I don't make time to listen to God.

» What noises fill your space and occupy your attention?

» Can you commit to a period of time today to just be silent? When?

During this time just listen. You will have to fight to listen, but do it. Sometimes I keep a journal out so I can bullet things off if they come to mind that I feel like I need to do. I often need to remove as many distractions as possible, too.

» **What can you do to stay more focused on listening?**

Also, I often find that going places help me see God and hear Him more clearly. These places need to be distraction free. For me it's anything outdoors—our backyard, going to the lake, going on a walk, our living room late at night or very early morning, etc.

» **Where's a place that you can hear God more clearly?**

Ok, you got this! Remember, if this is new for you, it will likely feel very forced.

» **Did you hear God say anything to your heart during this time?**

» **Anything else you are taking away from this time?**

Sabbath

**PRAISE GOD. REPENT OF SINS. ASK FOR OTHERS AND YOURSELF.
YIELD TO GOD. WAIT AND LISTEN.**

This isn't a day we will guide you through. It's a day just for you and Him—a day of rest (which isn't the same thing as a day of laziness).

» *What brings you rest that you will do today?*

» *How will you protect your Sabbath and keep it Holy (Exodus 20:8)?*

Come back and journal here about your day before you go to sleep.

» *What did you learn about God on your Sabbath?*

» *What did you learn about yourself?*

» *What do you need to do or not do next time to make for a more holy Sabbath?*

» *Anything else you learned or realized or noticed today?*

weekly plan

WEEK DAY	✓	ITEM(S) TO DO	OBSTACLES	SOLUTIONS
SUN				
MON				
TUES				
WED				
THUR				
FRI				
SAT				

FASTING

This week I will fast from:

_____

I am fasting from this because:

_____

In order to keep this fast, I need to:

_____

Week 4

Light Brings Freedom (Blow Out Third Candle)

The Greatest & Newest Things

Talents & Enough-ness

Dirty Feet Clean

Prayer with Others

Sabbath

Light Brings Freedom

PRAISE GOD. REPENT OF SINS. ASK FOR OTHERS AND YOURSELF.

YIELD TO GOD. WAIT AND LISTEN.

The Pharisees, the religious elite, frequently questioned Jesus. They wanted to trap Him; they wanted to stop Him. It seems that they felt equally outraged and threatened by Jesus.

» *Read John 1:1-18 and write out verse 5.*

The Pharisees weren't entirely unjustified in their confusion. They just didn't know. They weren't ready to believe. Hindsight is always 20/20, isn't it?

» *Have you ever been at a total loss for what God could be doing?*

I could go on for hours answering that question. God and I have such different ideas for how things should go!

BLOW OUT ONE CANDLE

(YOU SHOULD HAVE 4 LIT)

» What does John 1:12 say can happen for us?

» How would you define "receive Him...and believe in His name"?

» Have you "received Him"? Do you "believe in His name"? Share how this happened for you.

The whole process of coming to receive and believe is truly unbelievable. It's hard to even share about it. If you don't believe, it sounds like pure foolishness. Jesus and choosing to follow Him makes absolutely zero sense. It just doesn't.

A few years after I became a Christian I entered a huge season of doubt. I stopped going to Church, I stopped reading the Bible. I stopped praying. Instead, I explored every other religion out there. I wanted to find what was true. As I moved further and further from the Light and into darkness, one thing haunted me: What Jesus had done in me. I couldn't escape what His presence in my life had accomplished in me.

» Read again John 1:18 and also John 14:6-7 and write out what they say about knowing God.

Here's the truth, you won't ever know that you know that you know God is true. Not any more than you will know that you know that you know that the man who stands across from you on your wedding day will be forever faithful to you and the vows he speaks to you.

Faith is hard. God knew that and sent us Jesus. I know that sounds like a Sunday school answer and I'm sorry for that, but it is the truth.

Our crazy gracious Father saw our need to know Him and sent Jesus.

» *Since we can't see Jesus physically, how do we still get to experience Him?*

The more we know Jesus the more we will know our Father. We are 2,000-plus years too late to physically see Christ, but He has given us His Word. We get to know Him, Light of the world, every time we open His Word. We don't have to be in darkness any longer. His Word is our flashlight. That sounds so cheesy but I mean it. We know Him by knowing His Word, learning who He is and following the ways He has set for us to walk. We find Him along the way. His Spirit, our Helper, will guide us too. His light is free and always available.

» *Do things still feel dark for you? (It's OK to say yes.)*

» *How is your time in the Word? How often do you study or meditate on it?*

The Scriptures you have before you right now (not this book, the other really big book next to it), are your light. They are how you will know God. Put it before you all throughout the day, not just during this time of study.

» *Wrap up today by reading Joshua 1:5-9 and write out what you learn about God and His Word.*

My friend, I leave you with the same charge—"Do not turn from it (the Word of God) to the right hand or to the left, that you may have good success wherever you go...Be strong and courageous. Do not be frightened, and do not be dismayed, for the Lord your God is with you wherever you go."

- **Underline "Be strong and courageous"**

- **Cross out "Do not be frightened" and "Do not be dismayed"**

- **Underline "The Lord your God is with you wherever you go"**

This is truth, friend. Keep underlining and crossing out until you believe it just a smidge more today than you did yesterday.

WHAT SHOULD I DO?

How can you apply what you have heard today? (James 1:22)

_____

_____

_____

WHO SHOULD I TELL?

What is something you can share about today? Who should you share this with?

_____

_____

_____

SHARE WHAT GOD IS TEACHING YOU!

The Greatest and Newest Thing

PRAISE GOD. REPENT OF SINS. ASK FOR OTHERS AND YOURSELF.

YIELD TO GOD. WAIT AND LISTEN.

Prior to Jesus, there wasn't a lot of talk about love. Rules? Plenty. Regulations? You bet. Love? Not as much, not to the point of it feeling foremost.

» *Read the first command to love in Deuteronomy 6:5 and write it below:*

» *What were they to do with the commands? (v6-9)*

Some Jews took the commands literally and actually bound the Scripture at of these places mentioned in Deuteronomy 6. They are serious about memorizing and meditating on the Word of God. I'm not going to argue with their intent, because it really does not matter.

What we can for sure deduce is that God believed that following His commands was an expression of our love for Him. He desired for us to express this love all the time, not a moment was to be excluded.

Jesus comes and narrows it down to one commandment, the greatest of all. For the Jews, who surely felt the heavy weight of rules upon rules and commands, it must have been a relief. One commandment. The greatest of all.

» Read Mark 12:28-34 and John 13:34-35 and write out the commandments:

(You can also read Matthew 22:34-40 for another account of the Greatest Commandment.)

Define the following in your own words:

- **Love the Lord your God with all your heart.**

- **Love the Lord your God with all your soul.**

- **Love the Lord your God with all your mind.**

- **Love the Lord your God with all your strength.**

- **Love your neighbor as yourselves.**

We could break apart the Greek definitions of each word, but in many ways I think it complicates things for us today. His command is simple and doesn't need explaining, even if does need some time to identify more clearly.

To love is often harder than to serve or do or achieve. Loving is hard work and often takes great effort. There isn't an easy checklist for loving either. It's vague, but there's more freedom in it.

» Use the space below to brainstorm ways you could love God and others more fully.

WHAT SHOULD I DO?

How can you apply what you have heard today? (James 1:22)

WHO SHOULD I TELL?

What is something you can share about today? Who should you share this with?

SHARE WHAT GOD IS TEACHING YOU!

Talents and Enough-ness

PRAISE GOD. REPENT OF SINS. ASK FOR OTHERS AND YOURSELF.

YIELD TO GOD. WAIT AND LISTEN.

_____

_____

_____

_____

It happens nearly every time I sit across from a new client or talk with a woman after I speak somewhere: "I don't know what I'm supposed to do with my life. I feel like I have nothing to offer. I'm not enough." That's the summary of course, but the message is consistent. Their eyes tell me they believe they offer little value to this world. They feel they are not enough.

Enough. It's a hard word to define, let alone believe about ourselves. It doesn't matter how many self help books we absorb, we struggle to believe we are enough.

» **Do you struggle to believe you are enough? That your contribution to the world, or your world, is not enough?**

Today let's bring all our insecurities, our courage, and our dreams to Him. Let's trust that His plans are more than we could think or imagine (Isaiah 55:8-9). Let's see what God has to say about who we are and what we have to offer this world we live in.

» **Read Matthew 25:14-30 and make notes of what occurs below:**

I'm not much of a math girl, but there is great value in seeing some equations written out.

Fill out the chart below based off of this parable:

STARTED WITH	ACTION TAKEN	EARNED	TOTAL	FAITHFUL OVER...	SET OVER...
5					
2					
1					

This isn't a rich get richer story. This is a God's faithful get richer story. I say this with caution because in no way do I believe that wealth is a blessing from God. Living in America and having some worldview perspective, I think we can all agree that the monetarily rich aren't the most blessed. Life is easier, in some regards, when money isn't a stress. I know this first hand. Being able to pay your bills on time is a huge relief. The beep that chip card readers still causes my heart to beat faster because I remember a beep sound signaling that my card was declined just a decade ago. There is a feeling of relief when finances aren't an issue. However, that isn't what this story is really about.

» *What do you think this story is really about?*

Our talents, not just our finances, are the things God has entrusted to us. Our unique giftings, our spiritual gifts, our roles, our responsibilities, our people, etc.

» *List your talents:*

» *Which person do you connect with most in this parable? Why?*

I don't know what you feel like you are supposed to do with your life, or if you even know yet. I know many of us feel like one billion other people are already doing some variation of what we are doing or want to do. What we have to offer would be so lame in comparison or just another noise in the crowd. I struggle most in looking at the starting numbers five, two and one. I so often feel like the person with just 1 and think there is no way I could make something of what I'm holding.

» Look at your chart, what was the action the person with just one took? How do you do the same? (v18)

» Why do you think they hid?

» Why do you hide?

They lost everything and received the scorn of the Master all because they hid. It wasn't like they had just a short time to do it, verse 19 says the Master returned "after a long time."

In contrast, the person who had five, entrusted with much, and the person who had two, entrusted with little, were both given the same response from their Master, "I will set you over much." The starting numbers no longer mattered, but their faithfulness mattered much.

Fear and faith, our constant battle.

There is one passage I turn to every time I get scared. I'm pretty sure it's been in every study I've written and will be a part of anything I'm part of because its truth is simple and powerful.

The Israelites, oh those poor Israelites. We see it coming for them every time but forget how often we are just like them. So grateful the Lord doesn't give up on them, even if they have to learn His love the very hard way.

They had finally escaped slavery, on their way to freedom until this moment. In front of them a Sea and behind them Pharoah's army coming to take them back to slavery. It didn't look good. They began whining and asking, "WWHHHHYYYYYYY?????" It would be annoying to read except we totally get it! We do it too.

» Read Exodus 14:13-14 and write out what we should do and what the Lord will do.

God's got this, my friend. Whatever your dreams are or gifts are or talents you bring, He can use it. On your own, you are right: you are not enough, but He is. Your God is more than enough.

WHAT SHOULD I DO?

How can you apply what you have heard today? (James 1:22)

_____

_____

_____

WHO SHOULD I TELL?

What is something you can share about today? Who should you share this with?

_____

_____

_____

SHARE WHAT GOD IS TEACHING YOU!

Dirty Feet Clean

PRAISE GOD. REPENT OF SINS. ASK FOR OTHERS AND YOURSELF.

YIELD TO GOD. WAIT AND LISTEN.

_____

_____

_____

_____

Just last week we read about when Mary anointed Jesus's feet, and today we learn about when Jesus washed His disciples' feet. So sorry there is so much feet in this study. Kinda gross, I know, but we are just sticking with the text. The Bible doesn't always portray beautifully-staged pictures.

So onto stinky feet. As we learned with Jesus's anointing, feet were pretty gross in those days.

» Who was in charge of cleaning feet typically? Describe that person, as best you can imagine. It's OK to color outside the lines and use your imagination.

» Read John 13:1-20 and make any notes below:

» What do we learn about in verse 2?

Crazy, right? Jesus already knew, and He washed his feet anyway. He didn't try to change the course. He didn't spite Judas. As far as we can assume, He washed Judas's feet too.

> » *Imagine what that moment was like: Jesus washing Judas's feet. What might Jesus have thought and felt? What about Judas?*

The other disciples were assumably ignorant to the magnitude of that moment. Jesus, knowing what would happen, and Judas, knowing what He already had plans to do, were before one another. Judas's feet as dirty as his heart. Jesus's posture humble and serving Him even when He had every right not to.

> » *What can you learn from this moment between Jesus and Judas that's never described, but could be inferred ?*

And finally Peter. Hot mess, means-well Peter. He didn't want Jesus to wash his feet and then so quickly decides he wants Jesus to give him a total bath. I love his extreme heart probably because I relate to it a little too well.

> » *Do you connect with Peter? How would you have responded in that moment when Jesus kneeled before you?*

One last thing I don't want us to miss is the charge given to us.

> » *What charge does Jesus give us in response to what He has done? (v14-16)*

This seems like an odd charge. Some people take this figuratively and some literally. I think both are great ideas, although not all can apply it literally to each person you serve. Can you imagine walking up to your boss or Pastor with a bucket of water and taking off their shoes and start scrubbing!

We absolutely can apply this lesson and learn to serve those we lead.

» Who are people you lead?

» Go back next to each of their names and write one way you could serve them this week. For extra accountability, share this with a friend or add it to your calendar.

Excited to hear stories of you, awesome leaders, getting your hands dirty with stinky feet!

WHAT SHOULD I DO?

How can you apply what you have heard today? (James 1:22)

WHO SHOULD I TELL?

What is something you can share about today? Who should you share this with?

SHARE WHAT GOD IS TEACHING YOU!

Prayer with Others

**PRAISE GOD. REPENT OF SINS. ASK FOR OTHERS AND YOURSELF.
YIELD TO GOD. WAIT AND LISTEN.**

_____

_____

_____

_____

_____

Praying for others may not be something many of us struggle with. Hopefully all of our days are filled with whispered prayers for others. Today I want to encourage you to take it one or two steps further.

» *How do you feel about praying with others?*

If you feel anxious, know that you aren't alone. I'm asking you to trust me. I have friends who, at the thought of praying with others, have wanted to throw up or hyperventilate. They just couldn't do it. So they didn't for years.

I have a friend who prays the kind of prayers you'd be jealous of if you believed the lie that there is a "more spiritual" way to pray. The truth is she is only powerful with her prayers because she's confident talking with God because she does it so much. So you can imagine my shock when she told me that just a few years before, she had never prayed out loud before, by herself or with others. She was discipled by someone who used a Repeat-a-Prayer approach to help her learn to pray. Word for word, listening to her discipler pray a sentence, she would repeat that sentence back. In time as she let her insecurity go, she grew comfortable talking to God by herself.

I share her story to let you know that you are safe to pray right where you are. There isn't a right way or a better way. The best way is just your voice uttering the words in your heart to God. No matter how it sounds to you, it's beautiful to Him.

» *Have you ever prayed in a group or had someone pray over you? How did it make you feel?*

At the beginning of the study, I shared with you about my crazy fall season of health scares. I couldn't find the words to pray sometimes. I was literally held up by the prayers of my husband, friends, and Church.

Today I want you to experience prayer with others in two really powerful ways:

First, praying with others.

Matthew 18:20 says, "For where two or three are gathered in my name, there am I among them." This contrasts with many other Scriptures that talk about praying in secret (Matthew 6: 6) or not to be noticed. However, there are just as many, actually far more, examples of people praying in groups. However, we let these verses on praying in secret and our own insecurity keep us from praying with others.

» *Reach out to 1 - 3 people and ask them to get together to pray. Who did you reach out to? When are you gathering?*

» *Read and write out Acts 4:31 and share it with your prayer group.*

I'm praying your prayer time with others shakes some things up as it did for the people gathered in Acts 4.

Second, praying for someone else.

There is so much joy and love to be found as we begin praying for those around us. This can be done in many ways, find one that is best for you.

Here are a few suggestions:

- Send a text to someone(s) asking how you can pray for them. Do it and text them back that you did. Maybe even text back a prayer.
- Commit to praying for someone each day. Set an alarm to go off on your phone at a certain time to remind you.

- Ask the Spirit to show you people you could pray over that day. He might lead you to people you may have never noticed before or maybe see all the time.

- When people come in and out of your home, pray over them before they leave.

- If you have people in your home—roommates, parents, kids, spouse, etc.—pray over them.

» Who could you pray for today?

Come back at the end of the day and share!

» Who did you pray for? How did it go?

Sabbath

PRAISE GOD. REPENT OF SINS. ASK FOR OTHERS AND YOURSELF.

YIELD TO GOD. WAIT AND LISTEN.

This isn't a day we will guide you through. It's a day just for you and Jesus—a day of rest (which isn't the same thing as a day of laziness).

» *What brings you rest that you will do today?*

» *How will you protect your Sabbath and keep it Holy (Exodus 20:8)?*

Before you go to sleep, come back here and journal about your day.

» *What did you learn about God on your Sabbath?*

» *What did you learn about yourself?*

» *What do you need to do or not do to make for a more holy Sabbath?*

» *Anything else you learned or realized or noticed today?*

weekly plan

WEEK DAY	✓	ITEM(S) TO DO	OBSTACLES	SOLUTIONS
SUN				
MON				
TUES				
WED				
THUR				
FRI				
SAT				

FASTING

This week I will fast from:

_____

I am fasting from this because:

_____

In order to keep this fast, I need to:

_____

Week 5

His Word Brings Light

PRAISE GOD. REPENT OF SINS. ASK FOR OTHERS AND YOURSELF.

YIELD TO GOD. WAIT AND LISTEN.

I really struggle with not knowing and really hate not being able to make things right. Sure, I'll pray about it but if I'm being truthful, mostly I try to figure it out on my own. I'm not sure why I do this, but the doer in me likes to try to control as many things as possible. Tell me some of you relate to my ridiculousness. I've already picked out the title for a future book or study: *Control Freak Letting Go.* I feel certain it will be a big hit. One problem: I don't want to let go. Ha! Anyone else? You love your Pro and Con lists. You love brainstorming and strategy sessions. You love getting other people's advice or doing your due diligence research. Basically you love anything that makes you feel like you are being proactive.

We hate waiting. We hate not knowing.

And a lot of the time, with God, I feel like when I don't know what's going on, He is just keeping me in the dark. I don't like it one bit.

BLOW OUT ONE CANDLE

(YOU SHOULD HAVE 3 LIT)

» *Read and write out Psalm 119:105.*

I know that His Word lights my path. My brain gets that. I don't question it in technical terms. However, I totally lack implementing this belief.

» *Do you struggle with going to God's Word when you feel in the dark?*

Ok, we are going to break out of this together. We've shared about several fears or unknowns we have right now, and today we are going to take them to God's Word. We are going to put aside our pro/con lists, put aside our phones from calling our go-to people, and put aside our to-do lists. Today we are going to learn how to get Light from His Word.

» *Write down one fear or unknown you are dealing with right now.*

» *Google "Verses on (whatever you wrote above)" and write out all the references you find, look them up, and summarize them below.*

For example: Right now I'm really struggling with my obvious calling to my family but also my very felt calling to write and teach and lead. I believe He has called me to both but I deal with insecurity that I'm not cut out for either. I struggle with stress in trying to manage both. So for me, today, I would look up: "Verses on calling" or "verses on balance" or "verses on insecurity."

» *Pick one verse that speaks to you the most and write it out below.*

» Pick 3 places to post this verse and do that right now.

I just posted verses all over my house, and I'm so excited to let truth correct my faulty thinking. I have it on my bathroom mirror, above the water spout on my fridge, above the washer and dryer and in the front of my planner. I will see God's truth about 100 times a day.

» Where did you post your truth?

His Word will light our path. With time, as we hold His Word, the "lamp to our feet," our path will begin to lighten. He never promises we will see the final destination, but the journey doesn't have to be as overwhelming.

WHAT SHOULD I DO?

How can you apply what you have heard today? (James 1:22)

_____

_____

WHO SHOULD I TELL?

What is something you can share about today? Who should you share this with?

_____

_____

SHARE WHAT GOD IS TEACHING YOU!

The Best Bread and Wine Ever

PRAISE GOD. REPENT OF SINS. ASK FOR OTHERS AND YOURSELF.

YIELD TO GOD. WAIT AND LISTEN.

_____

_____

_____

_____

_____

It's happening: we are getting closer and I want to stall it. Each day the temptation to not write happens, as if it's not real if I don't write it. I want to write about Easter, I just don't want to write about all that occurs between today and Easter.

I hope our hearts break a little more this year than they have in years past. What had to happen because of sin is heartbreaking. Ugh, I hate this.

» Think back to Genesis 1, or go read it if you never have. Was this God's original plan? How might things be different today if sin had never entered the world?

It's hard to even imagine because sin is everywhere—we sin and our world is bursting with sin.

But there was a time when Adam and Eve literally walked with God (Genesis 3:8). Not our figurative walking with God we fight to experience and notice, but a literal walking with God in the Garden. That is so crazy cool. Instead of being in the Garden with all His people, we find His Son gathered around a Passover table with the 12 men He chose to follow Him.

» Read Matthew 26:17-25 and make notes about it below.

(To read other accounts, see Mark 14:12-25 and Luke 22:7-23.)

The Scriptures we will study for the next three weeks represent the final few days of Jesus on earth. This Passover meal occurred the Thursday before His crucifixion. In less than 24 hours from this moment, Jesus would die on the Cross.

>> *Pause on that for a moment. Write the numbers 1 through 24 below. Then circle the number 21. That was likely the amount of hours Jesus had left to live.*

For the next three weeks we will be creeping through His final 21 hours of life on earth.

>> *What did Jesus share with them? (v21) How did they respond? (v22) How did Judas respond? (v25)*

I'm not a violent person but I could so slap Judas right here. I cannot handle lies or fake people. Few things drive me as bonkers as deceit.

>> *How do you think you would've responded in this moment? (You know, if you weren't the Son of God. Ha!)*

>> *Let's keep going! Read Matthew 26:26-29 and make notes about it below.*

>> *What does the bread and blood represent?*

The commentary notes in my ESV Study Bible (Crossway Bibles) says, "Most likely the third of four cups at the Passover—the cup of blessing, or the cup of redemption—corresponding to God's third promise in Exodus 6:6, 'I will redeem you with an outstretched arm and with great acts of judgment.'"

» Turn to Exodus 6 and write out verses 6-8 below.

This is why He had to die. The only way to bring us out of burdens, to deliver us, to redeem us, and to take us to be His people was to give us His life. To bridge the massive gap between us and God.

Redemption.

At the time, the bread and wine that night would have little significance. All that would change in a day's time, and especially in a few days' time.

Redemption.

The bread, His body, and wine (or grape juice if you prefer), His blood, are our reminders of redemption.

Write out or summarize what the following verses teach you about redemption and your Redeemer. (Don't skip this part. I know we've already done a lot of work today. Keep pushing yourself. His Word brings life. You are worth this and so is He.)

• *Psalm 106:10*

• *Isaiah 41:14*

• *Isaiah 44:22*

• *Isaiah 51:10*

• *Isaiah 62:12*

- *Micah 6:4*

- *1 Corinthians 1:30-31*

- *Galatians 3:13*

- *Ephesians 1:7-10*

We use the word redemption when we finally get our way. When we've been wronged somehow and finally we've been vindicated.

Redemption for Jesus is the opposite of that—when He has been wronged, He makes everything right between us and Him. Redemption is His outstretched arms, the bread, and the blood that fell from His nail-pierced hands, the wine.

WHAT SHOULD I DO?

How can you apply what you have heard today? (James 1:22)

_____

_____

_____

WHO SHOULD I TELL?

What is something you can share about today? Who should you share this with?

_____

_____

_____

SHARE WHAT GOD IS TEACHING YOU!

I Don't Know Him

PRAISE GOD. REPENT OF SINS. ASK FOR OTHERS AND YOURSELF.

YIELD TO GOD. WAIT AND LISTEN.

Today's story is a familiar one for a couple of reasons—we've likely heard it before and we've also lived it out countless times ourselves.

» *Read Mark 14:26-31 and note what you learn below:*
(For additional accounts see: Matthew 26:30-35; Luke 22:31-34; John 13:36-38)

» *Have you ever, like Peter, felt like you would never deny Jesus?*

» *Have you ever turned away from Christ for a moment or a season? Like not just sinned, turned away, but actually denied to be a follower of Him? How did that feel?*

» *Read Mark 14:66-72 and note what you learn below:*
(For additional accounts see: Matthew 26:69-75; Luke 22:54-62; John 18:15-18)

He was so certain this wouldn't happen. Confident that not only would he never deny Christ, but that if he was charged for following Christ, he would be willing to die with Jesus. How quickly things can change when fear is pressing.

Some of us are in seasons where we are like Peter, denying Christ blatantly. These are hard places to get out of, and I urge you to confide these struggles with someone you can trust. Ask them to help you find your way back to belief in Jesus and out of the lies.

Most of us stand secure in our confidence in Christ. And why shouldn't we, persecution in America isn't a real thing. Not really. Turn on the news or do a quick google search and you can get an idea of what persecution looks like on a worldview level—beheadings, beating, children taken away, being burned alive, lost jobs, lost homes, imprisonment, etc. If people find a page of the Bible on you or hear you claim the name of Christ, you can be killed immediately.

We just don't experience persecution in America. We feel uncomfortable, but we don't very often experience our lives being threatened because of our connection to Christ, not like Peter.

» *What are ways you feel uncomfortable because of your connection with Christ? Be honest here. No shame. It is good to identify these things. What are situations where you feel uncomfortable to claim the name of Jesus?*

For me it's always in new situations when I don't feel like people know me or they have a seemingly more important position than I do. Basically when I'm insecure. I want to win people over to Jesus with my love, and in turn I can often deny Him in the process. It's so stupid.

Identify your top 3 places you tend to deny Christ with your actions, words or lack of words. Then write a game plan for how you could be more honest. Sometimes we want to be bold for Christ, when all we really need to do is just be honest about Christ. We have nothing to apologize for.

1.

2.

3.

WHAT SHOULD I DO?

How can you apply what you have heard today? (James 1:22)

_____

_____

_____

WHO SHOULD I TELL?

What is something you can share about today? Who should you share this with?

_____

_____

_____

SHARE WHAT GOD IS TEACHING YOU!

Questions and a Helper

PRAISE GOD. REPENT OF SINS. ASK FOR OTHERS AND YOURSELF.

YIELD TO GOD. WAIT AND LISTEN.

_____

_____

_____

_____

I hope you are loving our study of Scripture together and that God is speaking powerfully to you. If not, if it falls flat, ask Him to bring His Word to life to you! I am praying that for you.

Today I'm going to leave you on your own. I want you to practice some of the things we've applied in this study so far. I'll give you some basic guiding, but I want you to fill in the blanks. You can do it. Ask Him to lead you. I can't wait to hear what He shows you!

We are going to look at two different things Jesus said during the Passover meal He shared with His chosen 12.

» Read John 14:1-14 and note what occurs.

» What does Jesus teach about Heaven? (v2-4)

» Write out verse 6. Then write your own definitions for each of the descriptors Jesus gave Himself.

» What did Philip ask in verse 8? Have you asked similar questions? Do you have those questions now?

» How did Jesus respond when asked for proof that He is God? (v10-11)

» What does Jesus say we would be able to do? (v12-14) Do you honestly believe that? Have you ever experienced this happening? Why or why not?

Don't you love how patient Jesus is with all our questions? He isn't afraid of them. Know that it is safe to bring all your questions to Him.

» Do you have any questions for Him? Ask Him, then actively look for His answers.

I've tried to phase myself out of this study on a lot of days, so you could see you can pursue Him on your own—just you and His Word open. You don't need to have a Bible study. Hear me, I see great value in Bible studies (obviously, it's what I do for a living) but I am begging God that you know that His Word is enough and it's all because of the gift He has given us!

» Read John 14:15-31 and note what occurs.

You've got this because the Spirit, your Helper, "He will teach you all things and bring to your remembrance all that I (Jesus) have said to you." I'm not going to walk you through this next portion of Scripture that you just read. You do it. Look at the text and chew on it. Read through it slowly and ask it questions. Find verses that support or contrast what's said. Define words that stand out to you. Write questions out that you want answers to.

Your turn to study His Word with your Helper...

WHAT SHOULD I DO?

How can you apply what you have heard today? (James 1:22)

_____

_____

_____

WHO SHOULD I TELL?

What is something you can share about today? Who should you share this with?

_____

_____

_____

SHARE WHAT GOD IS TEACHING YOU!

Prayer Walk

PRAISE GOD. REPENT OF SINS. ASK FOR OTHERS AND YOURSELF.

YIELD TO GOD. WAIT AND LISTEN.

There are many official prayer walks you can do I am sure. This is a little different from a "walk around Jericho" march, much more low key.

A year after I became a Christian and the summer before my senior year in high school, a woman I admired so much invited me to a prayer walk at our high school. I was passionate to make my final year at our school mean something for God. I was a new believer and know very little about what following Jesus looked like.

I showed up eager to pray and also totally insecure. I had never prayer walked before and had no clue what it might be like. Now, 15 years later, I have learned there isn't a right or wrong way to prayer walk. You just walk and pray. Pretty simple! Ha!

However, she taught me a prayer tool I had never heard of before and still have never heard taught.

» Read and write out 1 Thessalonians 5:17.

This can feel overwhelming, right? How do we pray without stopping? Honestly, I'm not sure. But I know most of it has to do with keeping the mindset of constant communication with God.

Back to my first prayer walk. Mrs. Bridgewater gathered a bunch of teenagers in our stinky cafeteria and instructed us on what this prayer walk would look like. She said, *"Use the things already around you and let them prompt you to pray."*

Next she modeled it for us. She walked over to the trash cans and prayed something like, "Lord, may you remove all the wasteful things in this school, all trash, the things that don't honor you. Would you throw out all sin in this place. All relationships that don't honor you. Cease all words that don't bring you glory..." Then she walked to the stage at the front of the cafeteria and prayed something like, "Lord Jesus may those who know you use all that they do here as a platform to share about you. May their lives lead others to You. May they not see their own glory..." Then she walked over to the soda and snack machines and prayed something like, " May the things these students put into themselves cause them to know you more. May no unwholesome thing enter them Jesus..."

Since that day I use this tool all the time. The beautiful thing about it is that you can too—it can be done anywhere and anytime! You can pray out loud or in your head, that part doesn't matter. Just talk to God and let the things around you lead you.

You can pray literally too—walk your street or apartment complex and pray over the people in each home as you pass. Walk around at work and pray over each area that other people occupy as you walk past their space.

» **How are you going to apply this today?**

Come back later today and share!

» **How was your prayer walk today?**

Sabbath

PRAISE GOD. REPENT OF SINS. ASK FOR OTHERS AND YOURSELF.

YIELD TO GOD. WAIT AND LISTEN.

This isn't a day we will guide you through. It's a day just for you and Him—a day of rest (which isn't the same thing as a day of laziness).

» *What brings you rest that you will do today?*

» *How will you protect your Sabbath and keep it Holy (Exodus 20:8)?*

Come back and journal here about your day before you go to sleep.

» *What did you learn about God on your Sabbath?*

» *What did you learn about yourself?*

» *What do you need to do or not do next time to make for a more holy Sabbath?*

» *Anything else you learned or realized or noticed today?*

weekly plan

WEEK DAY	✓	ITEM(S) TO DO	OBSTACLES	SOLUTIONS
SUN				
MON				
TUES				
WED				
THUR				
FRI				
SAT				

FASTING

This week I will fast from:

_____

I am fasting from this because:

_____

In order to keep this fast, I need to:

_____

Week 6

He Leads the Blind

PRAISE GOD. REPENT OF SINS. ASK FOR OTHERS AND YOURSELF.

YIELD TO GOD. WAIT AND LISTEN.

_____

_____

_____

_____

_____

I hope you have loved following Jesus on His final days. Loved might be a strange word, because it's heartbreaking too. To observe Him being betrayed and questioned is heart wrenching. He never once gave up because He knew what He needed to do. He kept going. He is always able.

> **» Read Isaiah 42:16 and write it out.**

Go back and circle every use of the word "I" in reference to God.

> **» How many times is God referenced?**

> **» What does it say about us ("they")?**

BLOW OUT ONE CANDLE

(YOU SHOULD HAVE 2 LIT)

The unknowns aren't awesome, but maybe they're intended. Maybe they are actually gifts and opportunities to learn that His way is better.

» *Share about a time you forced your way, even if it wasn't best?*

There's evidence all throughout Scripture of God letting his people go down other paths.

» *Who, in the Word, made choices that weren't honoring to God?*

You aren't alone in dishonoring God. We aren't alone. I take such comfort in that for some reason.

Two questions remain for all of us:

1. How do I get off this wrong path?
2. How do I get on the right path?

Thankfully the answer is the same to both: Jesus. Our go-to church answer, Jesus, is the only response. Well actually the full Trinity: Jesus, Holy Spirit, and Father God.

Read Romans 8:24-28

» *What is our job? (v24-25)*

Hoping and waiting. Ugh. Those aren't fun at all.

» *What happens when we hope and wait patiently? (v28)*

When we do not know we can trust in the Spirit to intercede for us, we can trust that God can work anything for good!

» What are some things in your life that you just don't feel confident that any good could come from them?

» Go back and write on top of those words, "ALL THINGS!"

I'm not sure when we started to believe that God couldn't handle our mess-ups. That we needed to get things together to come to Him or keep things together to stay in His favor. Our heads know He loves us but we don't trust Him to really love us when we take a path that wasn't His.

» Flip back to Isaiah 42:16 and bullet out what God says He will do:

The last one stings the most: "I will not forsake them." I think the reason we struggle to trust God is simply because we struggle to trust. Again, our heads likely believe it is true because we know He has said it, but our hearts (and likely our way of living) doesn't feel the same. We've been hurt enough times to know better. So we trust Him with our heads and protect our hearts even from Him. Vulnerability, even with God, is a terrifying thing. Trusting Him is something we desperately want to do but struggle with daily.

Today let's take steps towards trusting Him.

» Wrap up today with praying. Get on your knees if possible; if not, sit with hands opened in your lap. Confess to God any areas of not trusting Him. Imagine each of those areas in your hands. Ask Him to give you the faith to hand it over to Him. If you are ready, hand them over. Envision Him taking them. Tell Him you trust Him to not forsake you.

One final note that I know isn't for everyone. I know some of you have been burned in serious ways and others in smaller ways, and trusting Him doesn't come easily because you feel justified in your opinion that He has let you down. I would encourage you to do a couple of things:

- *Really think through your motives and circumstance. Was He really out to get you or could He have been protecting you all along? Or could He possibly be using that situation to make you stronger or to bring others to Him? A large majority of our "Not fair, God!" moments are really just us being upset that we didn't get our way. (Not everyone will be able to answer yes to this.)*

- *Keep surrendering this to God. Keep talking to Him about it.*

- *Stop talking about it to others who fuel the fire of unbelief. You might want to give permission to those you typically vent to, to tell you to shut up next time you get at it again.*

- *It might be helpful to find a Christian counselor to help you work through these issues. I know we don't like to do this as Christians. Forgiveness should be enough. We have the Spirit, our great Counselor, so we don't need someone else we don't know. We don't need to dredge it up. Here's the truth: It's up. You may think it's not but if it's affecting your ability to trust God or others, get help now. Don't wait.*

Thank you for trusting me today. I know it wasn't easy work, but it was worth it work. You have a Father who loves you so very much—He sent His Son for you!

WHAT SHOULD I DO?

How can you apply what you have heard today? (James 1:22)

_____

_____

WHO SHOULD I TELL?

What is something you can share about today? Who should you share this with?

_____

_____

SHARE WHAT GOD IS TEACHING YOU!

It's OK to be Honest

PRAISE GOD. REPENT OF SINS. ASK FOR OTHERS AND YOURSELF.

YIELD TO GOD. WAIT AND LISTEN.

We often see Jesus retreat to be alone. We have all heard the Lord's prayer that He modeled for us. However, here, we finally get a peek into His communication with the Father. These are some of the most sacred and vulnerable words spoken in the entire Bible, in my personal opinion. This account has completely changed the way I talk to God, especially when things are hard. I hope you find great honesty in your prayers today. Freedom to remove all pretense. He doesn't need our fake belief that all is going to be awesome. He just needs our trust in Him and His will.

Read Matthew 26:36-46 and write out the prayers of Jesus next to the reference:

(For other accounts, read: Mark 14:32-42; Luke 22:39-46)
- ***v39***

- ***v42***

- ***v44***

We are going to ignore the disciples' lack of involvement in this moment and just focus on Jesus and what He experienced.

» *Turn to Luke 22:39-46 and note what additional things we learn from this account.*

» *What do these two accounts tell you about Jesus's emotional state in His final hours?*

Fully man. Fully God.

Sometimes the pictures or movies portray Jesus as this cool and calm guy. Like He peaceably walked through this whole thing because the Son of God would never push against all that was happening. We are afraid, maybe, if we talk about Jesus asking to not go to the cross and being so anxious that He sweat blood, it makes Him less of a Savior.

» *Does it affect how you see Him as Savior to know He didn't want to do it, even if He was willing? How so?*

» *Are there some areas you could be more like Jesus and pray more honestly?*

Back to those disciples.

» *Why do you think they keep falling asleep?*

» *Do you feel like you've been falling asleep on Jesus? How so?*

» What are ways you need to wake up? What is something you could do to set some alarms for yourself—literally and/or figuratively.

With your remaining time pray as honestly as you ever have. Go back to the list you created above and repeat the prayer your Savior once uttered. It's OK to tell your Father, *"Father, if you are willing, remove this cup from me. Nevertheless, not my will, but yours, be done."* (v42)

WHAT SHOULD I DO?

How can you apply what you have heard today? (James 1:22)

_____

_____

_____

WHO SHOULD I TELL?

What is something you can share about today? Who should you share this with?

_____

_____

_____

SHARE WHAT GOD IS TEACHING YOU!

A Kiss on the Cheek

PRAISE GOD. REPENT OF SINS. ASK FOR OTHERS AND YOURSELF.

YIELD TO GOD. WAIT AND LISTEN.

We are getting further into the study and closer to the Cross. I hope you are gaining confidence in studying the Scripture. Slowing down and taking note of the details already given to you. Today I'm going to leave you on your own again. At the risk of sounding cheesy, you aren't alone—you have a Helper, the Holy Spirit. Ask Him to show you whatever you need to see. I'm going to give you a few prompts, but other than that it's all you and Him today. Enjoy!

Pick one of the accounts of Jesus's Betrayal and Arrest: Matthew 26:47-56; Mark 14:43-50; Luke 22:47-53; John 18:1-11.

- **Make general notes of what occurred.**

- **Who was there?**

- **What happened?**

- *How did people respond?*

- *What was shocking?*

- *What are things you never noticed before?*

What you're doing is observing Scripture—looking at it not for head knowledge or holiness, rather simply to know Jesus.

Now let's try to understand it more, many call this interpreting Scripture. This is where you look at what you've read and start to ask it questions. Here are some that I ask:

» **Are there any words that stand out?** *Look them up and write out definitions (from an online English or Greek dictionary)*

» **Are any emotions expressed? By who? What does it mean?**

» **What were people's motives when they did certain things? Why did they do that?**

» **You try. What are some questions you could ask this text?**

Finally, we always want to apply what we've read. We've been doing that each day with our Doer of the Word challenge. You can fill that section out now.

WHAT SHOULD I DO?

How can you apply what you have heard today? (James 1:22)

WHO SHOULD I TELL?

What is something you can share about today? Who should you share this with?

SHARE WHAT GOD IS TEACHING YOU!

A Savior or a Murderer

PRAISE GOD. REPENT OF SINS. ASK FOR OTHERS AND YOURSELF.

YIELD TO GOD. WAIT AND LISTEN.

_____

_____

_____

_____

_____

I can't image how Jesus remained standing. How He didn't just pull rank on them all and play the "I'm the Son of God and I can do whatever I want" card. He withstood so much. Too much.

>> *Read Mark 15:6-16 and make note of what you observe.*
(You can read other accounts in Matthew 27:15-23; Luke 23:18-15; John 18:33-40)

It was between Jesus, who had done "no evil" according to Pilate (v14), and Barabbas, a committed murderer. There was actually a moment the people could've saved Jesus.

>> *Why do you think they chose to free Barabbas and demand that Jesus be crucified?*

>> *What do you suppose Jesus was thinking and feeling as this occurred?*

This passage always makes me wonder what I choose over Jesus? How often I send Him to the Cross for my own selfish reasons.

> **» Spend the rest of today asking God, "What do I choose over you?" Don't rush it. Really consider this. Write down what you realize. Ask God to forgive you. Ask your Helper, Holy Spirit, to help you choose Christ. Maybe even put together a plan. You have plenty of time and space. Choose Christ.**

WHAT SHOULD I DO?

How can you apply what you have heard today? (James 1:22)

_____

_____

_____

WHO SHOULD I TELL?

What is something you can share about today? Who should you share this with?

_____

_____

_____

SHARE WHAT GOD IS TEACHING YOU!

Ask for Prayer

PRAISE GOD. REPENT OF SINS. ASK FOR OTHERS AND YOURSELF.

YIELD TO GOD. WAIT AND LISTEN.

This day might be hard for a lot of us. Most of us women love being there for others but we hardly ever want to burden people with our issues.

Not today. Today we invite people in.

I have only one rule on this—it has to be a prayer request *for you.*

That just made you cringe a little, didn't it? Whenever I host a Bible study, I also have people fill out prayer request cards each week and I tell them the requests can only be about them—not their kids, or their job, or their sister's neighbor's dog. Nothing unspoken either. Specific and vulnerable requests.

» What do you need prayer for? (Specific and vulnerable)

» Who are 1 to 3 people that you could send these requests to?

» Do that right now. Text them and then put a check next to their name once you have sent it.

I'm so proud of you. I know it's hard to ask for prayer.

If it makes you feel better, I just did it myself (felt a little convicted by this idea). I'm 10 days from the final deadline for writing this study and still have quite a bit of work to do. So I made a list of 10 people I could get to pray for 10 days. I sent them each a text and asked them to pray. I also included some of the parts of this process I'm insecure in. I need their prayers because I need Jesus to accomplish this. I don't want it to be of my own efforts. I want this to ooze Jesus for you.

Sabbath

PRAISE GOD. REPENT OF SINS. ASK FOR OTHERS AND YOURSELF. YIELD TO GOD. WAIT AND LISTEN.

This isn't a day we will guide you through. It's a day just for you and Him—a day of rest (which isn't the same thing as a day of laziness).

» *What brings you rest that you will do today?*

» *How will you protect your Sabbath and keep it Holy (Exodus 20:8)?*

Come back and journal here about your day before you go to sleep.

» *What did you learn about God on your Sabbath?*

» *What did you learn about yourself?*

» *What do you need to do or not do next time to make for a more holy Sabbath?*

» *Anything else you learned or realized or noticed today?*

weekly plan

WEEK DAY	✓	ITEM(S) TO DO	OBSTACLES	SOLUTIONS
SUN				
MON				
TUES				
WED				
THUR				
FRI				
SAT				

FASTING

This week I will fast from:

_____

I am fasting from this because:

_____

In order to keep this fast, I need to:

_____

Week 7

Proclaim His Excellencies

PRAISE GOD. REPENT OF SINS. ASK FOR OTHERS AND YOURSELF.

YIELD TO GOD. WAIT AND LISTEN.

_____

_____

_____

_____

What Jesus endured will get harder to bear this week as we go to the cross.

(YOU SHOULD HAVE 1 LIT)

The amazing part of all of it is that He chose to still go to the cross. He chose to endure all of it for one reason.

> **» Read 1 Peter 2:9 and write it out.**

All of this was because He wanted us out of darkness and into light.

Define the descriptors God has for us:

- *Chosen:*

- *Royal:*

- *Holy:*

- *His Own:*

And He doesn't leave it at who we are, but He tells us what we are called to.

» *What does God say our job is?*

I'm not sure when we became such silent people. We are afraid to offend, so we stay silent. We want so badly to be relevant, so we stay silent because we aren't cool like that. We don't want to step on anyone's toes, so we choose tolerance and remain silent.

Now, some of us do a little more than proclaim: we scream our opinions or badger people. All we share on social media is very spiritual things. We are brave and bold online because we don't see the people reading our words. Or maybe we click forward on every single spiritual email that comes across our Inbox. Or we make it our mission to tell every single person about Jesus without even listening to their story or noticing their needs first.

Where do you fall? (Mark with X.)

Silent————————————— **Proclaim God**————————————**Screaming**

» What does "proclaim His excellencies" even mean?

I translate this phrase as: to brag about how awesome God is. Social media is a beautiful tool for this. I felt convicted by this and decided to share something on social media right now, picture of some favorite things in front of me: this study, chocolate cake, coffee, a sunset, a cool breeze (miracle in Texas), and His Word. These are good gifts. I know it because other moments of this week have not been as ideal. So today, this moment, I proclaim His goodness.

Use this Lent season to seek out opportunities to tell people about Jesus.

» Right now what can you thank God for?

» Who could you share those things with?

Go do it. No time like the present.

WHAT SHOULD I DO?

How can you apply what you have heard today? (James 1:22)

WHO SHOULD I TELL?

What is something you can share about today? Who should you share this with?

SHARE WHAT GOD IS TEACHING YOU!

@sacredholidays   #sacredholidays

A Bloody Mess

PRAISE GOD. REPENT OF SINS. ASK FOR OTHERS AND YOURSELF.

YIELD TO GOD. WAIT AND LISTEN.

Today we are going to try to follow along, step-by-step with Jesus. We want to know what He felt from His perspective. This isn't just another thing in the history books; this was the final moments of Jesus's life. The final words spoken to Jesus. His final things to see. Let's look at it from His perspective. I think it will change things for both of us.

» *For context, review and summarize what happened in Matthew 27:15-23.*

He had just been chosen, instead of a convicted murderer, to be crucified for no reason. Pilate actually said, "What evil has he done?"

» *Read Matthew 27:24-26 and write out verse 25.*

They wanted His blood on them, not just them but their children. Our sin, our separation, our curse. This is insanity.

» *Write out God's response to His blood stained people in Isaiah 1:18.*

Even when we stand there, hands stained with blood because we want our own way, our Father turns our sin-stained souls to the purest of white.

» What did Pilate do to Jesus before releasing Him? (Matthew 27:26)

We can almost miss it or see it as nothing if we go too quickly. The passivity of the text almost makes it sound like just a reprimand if we don't understand what scourging means.

This isn't something we are familiar with today. The ESV Study Bible describes it this way: *"Roman flogging was a horrifically cruel punishment. Those condemned to it were tied to a post and beaten with a leather whip that was interwoven with pieces of bone and metal, which tore through skin and tissue, often exposing bones and intestines. In many cases, the flogging itself was fatal. The Romans scourged Jesus nearly to death so that he would not remain alive on the cross after sundown."*

» Draw a picture of what was used to beat Jesus. You can use the description above or search the internet to find images to determine how to draw it. I know this seems like an odd activity, but I want us to visualize this moment as best we can.

He took this beating. His back literally ripped open for us. I can't even fathom this kind of pain. Bones exposed. Tradition said that just one more lashing, and death was imminent.

» What might have been going on in Jesus's mind as He was scourged/flogged?

» What is the most painful thing you've experienced? How do you think this compares to what Jesus experienced in that moment?

The worst is yet to come. His punishment is just getting started.

» *Read Matthew 27:27-31 and list out each thing the soldiers did to Jesus.*

All of that for no reason at all. The "whole battalion" of soldiers typically referred to 150-200 men. The grown men had nothing better to do than these things to Jesus.

Mind you He'd already been beaten up to near death, and now this. What a mess.

» *How do you imagine Jesus felt physically during this time?*

» *What thoughts and feelings do you suppose Jesus had during this mock-fest?*

With just a word He could've stopped it all. We've seen Him show His power in far greater ways, to stop this would've been so easy for Him.

» *Read and write out all of Isaiah 53:5-7.*

» *Go back and circle every word that was a physical pain Christ endured for you.*

All of it He endured for you to have peace and to be healed (v5).

He took every lash. History says there were 39 lashings (back and forth whippings). 39 times that whip of dried bones and sharp rock dug across His back. He could've stopped them at any point and He didn't.

He endured clothes being ripped off His torn open skin and stood there, before more than one hundred soldiers. He was naked for you.

Then they thought it would be funny to dress Him like a king. So they took your naked Savior with skin not just bloody, but ripped open, and they put a robe on Him. Not as a spa or hotel might offer, but to remind Him of how unlike a King He really was. They made Him a mock crown of out thorns and pressed it deep into His skull.

More blood, more unnecessary blood.

Then they spit on Him. They looked at Jesus and despised Him so much not just to mock Him but to spit on Him. Complete disdain and disrespect.

They handed Him a reed to hold and then used it to beat Him over His thorn-covered head.

Such a bloody mess.

Then it just ends. It seems the soldiers had no purpose, no goal in mind for this treatment. No reason. It wasn't a sentenced punishment. Just soldiers having some fun. On to the next thing.

» *Why do you think the soldiers did that?*

» *What do you imagine was going through Jesus's head? Think of all the things you've learned about Jesus over the past few weeks as you answer this question. There isn't a right or wrong answer, we are just imagining.*

This wasn't an easy day—a bloody mess. It would be easier to turn our heads or not look too closely because we don't really want to know. We like the pictures of resurrected Jesus a lot more than this picture. But we need to remember what He did for us. It wasn't a little spanking, or even severe beating. He endured total abandonment and mocking. His suffering wasn't just physical, it was emotional.

» *Have you ever had someone say something that hurt worse than a slap?*

I feel certain that the worst part, as horrid as it was, wasn't the flogging. The worst part was the rejection. To look into the eyes of ones you love so much and have them hate you is unbearable.

» *Do you relate to this on your own level? How has it made you feel to love and only receive complete rejection or abuse in return?*

WHAT SHOULD I DO?

How can you apply what you have heard today? (James 1:22)

_____

_____

_____

WHO SHOULD I TELL?

What is something you can share about today? Who should you share this with?

_____

_____

_____

SHARE WHAT GOD IS TEACHING YOU!

Forsaken

PRAISE GOD. REPENT OF SINS. ASK FOR OTHERS AND YOURSELF.

YIELD TO GOD. WAIT AND LISTEN.

Today we are getting a headstart. Use what you focus on today to settle in on your heart and mind over the next few days. The cross isn't typically something that grieves us. Instead we like to decorate our homes and ourselves with it. The symbol of the cross is now more of our club's brand, as opposed to the place our sins took our God to His death.

» *When you see a cross, what do you typically think about?*

I hope today that we can bring some reverence back to the cross as we remember what happened that day.

Before we go to the Cross, I want us to come to it with better understanding.

» *Read Hebrews 9:22 and write it out below.*

We don't get this concept of needing a blood sacrifice for sins. In those days it was the practice of the Jews. They regularly made sacrifices of animals for sins. You even see it in other cults or religions, where they sacrifice animals or even people. Our culture has gotten so far from this, which is healthy in so many ways. However, we don't see sin or a need for penance. We live in a society where every kid gets a trophy and everyone is special. We don't know how to handle conflict, so we avoid it. Our society has become so self-centered and so tolerant that we have a hard time seeing our need for the blood sacrifice.

> » *Would you agree with this? Do you struggle with this idea? Do you think others, who don't claim Jesus, struggle with this concept?*

The meaning of the cross gets lost on us when it comes to the sacrifice, because we just can't even relate. The meaning of the cross is lost on us because the pain and brutality of the cross is nothing compared to what we see in PG-13 movies nowadays.

Today I want you to fight to see the meaning and the purpose of the Cross. You are going to study most of it on your own today. May your reading today feel more like a conversation with Christ. Ask Him to show you what He did and why, and how that relates to your life and those around you.

Read Matthew 27:33-56 through once, then answer the questions below:

> » **Where did they go? (v33)**

> » **What did they offer Jesus to drink? What did He do? (v34)**

> » **What did they do with Jesus? (v35)**

> » **What did they do with His things? (v35)**

> » **Who was present at the cross? (v32, 38, 39, 41, 47, 56)**

> » **What were the final words Jesus heard spoken to Him? (v39-40, 42-43)**

» What happened in nature? (v45)

» What was the first thing Jesus said on the cross? Why did He say it? (v46)

» What was He offered again? What was different about it this time? (v46, 34)

» What was the last thing Jesus did on the Cross? (v50)

» What happened next? (v51-54)

A lot happened in just a few verses, actually everything happened. Our lives and the world were never the same because of that day.

We could go into the details of the excruciating pain that Jesus endured that day for us. I encourage you to go and do some research. Also watch some of the movies about Jesus, like the Passion of the Christ or Son of God. It's a beautiful way to visually experience what that day might have looked like. There are also many articles you can search to learn more about the pain of being crucified.

We are going to try something that will be easy for some of you and challenging for others, like me. We are going to sketch out the scene. By sketch I mean stick figure at best, unless you are an artist and it's more fun for you to be fancy. By doing this, the whole scene is further engrained into our minds. Use the answers from above to draw it out. Do voice bubbles to express what people said. Draw and label those there. Don't use what you've seen in the movies or picture Bibles, just draw it out exactly as the Word describes.

» Sketch out the scene of the cross below:

» *What's your biggest thought when staring at this picture?*

» *What do you imagine was going through Jesus's head the entire time?*

» *Why didn't He stop it, especially after hearing it would cause others to believe? (v42)*

» *Why did Christ have to die on the Cross?*

» *Read Romans 3:23-26 and write out the parts that answer the previous question.*

» *Read and write out 2 Corinthians 5:21.*

Our sin nailed Him there so that *"we might become the righteousness of God."*

Today we looked at Jesus on the cross and those around Him. Tomorrow we will go to the Cross.

(BONUS) If you have time or are able to come back, read the other accounts in the other gospels (Mark 15:21-41; Luke 23:26-49; John 19:16-37). Mark below any additional pieces to this story.

WHAT SHOULD I DO?

How can you apply what you have heard today? (James 1:22)

WHO SHOULD I TELL?

What is something you can share about today? Who should you share this with?

SHARE WHAT GOD IS TEACHING YOU!

Dead and Buried

PRAISE GOD. REPENT OF SINS. ASK FOR OTHERS AND YOURSELF. YIELD TO GOD. WAIT AND LISTEN.

_____

_____

_____

_____

This is typically a day of grief and unknown. Jesus had already died. It was over. What we are learning about today actually occurred immediately following His death, when we typically focus on the cross on Good Friday. So today before we get started on our Scripture, let's think about that day. We know from our reading yesterday that this day in between the crucifixion and the resurrection was the sabbath, a day of rest.

» *With Jesus dead, what do you think was going through the disciples' minds this day?*

» *With Jesus dead, what do you think was going through the Pharisees' minds this day?*

» *With Jesus dead, what do you think was going through Pilate's mind?*

» With Jesus dead, what do you think was going through Mary's, Jesus' mom, mind?

There are so many questions I have. I wish I could know more. I wish I could know what was going through their minds and hearts. We are nearly 2,000 years removed from this day and it feels like longer because the story seems so far off. These were real people though, not just characters in another best selling fiction book. Each of these people witnessed Jesus's life, the mockery He endured, the bloody mess, His crucifixion and then His burial.

Today's Scripture is short, so I'm going to ask you to read each Gospel's account of it. For the first one, write down everything that happens, then for the others, write down only the new information.

- **Matthew 27:57-61**

- **Mark 15:42-47**

- **Luke 23:50-56**

- **John 19:38-42**

He was really dead. Not dead and risen again like we see in the movies. This wasn't a "He died on the surgery table and a few minutes later the doctors revived Him." There were no doctors. There was no one able or trying to bring Him back to life. It was done.

Jesus was dead and buried.

WHAT SHOULD I DO?

How can you apply what you have heard today? (James 1:22)

_____

_____

_____

WHO SHOULD I TELL?

What is something you can share about today? Who should you share this with?

_____

_____

_____

SHARE WHAT GOD IS TEACHING YOU!

Prayers of Repentance

PRAISE GOD. REPENT OF SINS. ASK FOR OTHERS AND YOURSELF.

YIELD TO GOD. WAIT AND LISTEN.

Today is Good Friday. My husband always laughs at me because I get Good Friday and Black Friday confused every single time. Even now as I just wrote the words "Good Friday" I had to double check to make sure I had it right. I feel like Black Friday (day after Thanksgiving) should be called Good Friday because the sales are amazing and Good Friday should be called Black Friday because it's heartbreaking when we realize, like we did yesterday, what Jesus did on the cross for us. The good part comes on Sunday; without it, Friday was just a horrid occurrence. (Feel free to laugh at me.)

Today we look at the cross and we think of the reason He is there.

BLOW OUT ONE CANDLE

(YOU SHOULD HAVE NONE LIT)

» Why did Jesus have to go to the cross?

» Read and write out Romans 4:25.

Our sin is what nailed Jesus to that cross.

» Do you deal with shame over past sins or current ones?

» Read Luke 5:27-32 and write out verse 31-32.

Your perfection isn't what Jesus came for because it's not something you can pull off. So let's stop trying. He didn't come for those who had it all together, the seemingly "healthy." He came for you and me, "the sick." So let's come to Him sick by confessing and be willing to get healthy by repenting.

» Use the following page to confess any sin in your life. This can be sins that have crept up today and also sin that seems to continuously pop up again and again. Give this time; don't rush. Ask the Spirit to show you things you cannot see that separate you from Him.

Now go back to each of those things and ask God to show you how to turn away from those things. List out some of the turning back to God ideas that He gives you. Then ask Him to help you make these a reality. You might even want to take a picture of this part and send it to some of your most trusted friends.

Friend, you are so loved today. I hope you see His love and grace towards you.

» Read and write out 1 John 1:9 and underline what God does.

I hope you were able to notice all four things that are said of God:

He is faithful (He hasn't given up on you, even if you have)

He is just (His justice is different than we'd imagine)

He forgives our sins (every sin is marked forgiven)

He cleanses us from all unrighteousness (not some)

» Finally, read and write out Luke 23:34.

Even as He hung on the cross, the pain so immense we can never relate, He cared about forgiveness. Under that kind of torture, the rest of us would've caved and wanted relief. The only relief Jesus was after was the burden of unforgiven sin and shame.

» One more thing: write forgiven in giant letters over that cross.

Forgiven. That's who you are. You don't have to hide your sin. Take it to Him. Turn from it and turn to Him. Let His justice bring about forgiveness. No shame. No more hiding. His cross abolishes shame and brings forgiveness.

Sabbath

PRAISE GOD. REPENT OF SINS. ASK FOR OTHERS AND YOURSELF.

YIELD TO GOD. WAIT AND LISTEN.

This isn't a day we will guide you through. It's a day just for you and Him—a day of rest (which isn't the same thing as a day of laziness).

» *What brings you rest that you will do today?*

» *How will you protect your Sabbath and keep it Holy (Exodus 20:8)?*

Come back and journal here about your day before you go to sleep.

» *What did you learn about God on your Sabbath?*

» *What did you learn about yourself?*

» *What do you need to do or not do next time to make for a more holy Sabbath?*

» *Anything else you learned or realized or noticed today?*

Week 8

He is Alive! (Light All Seven Candles)

He is Alive!

PRAISE GOD. REPENT OF SINS. ASK FOR OTHERS AND YOURSELF.

YIELD TO GOD. WAIT AND LISTEN.

_____

_____

_____

_____

_____

Happy Easter! He is Risen!!!!!!!!!!!

Today isn't awesome because you get Cadbury eggs again or get to finally show off that new dress you found. Today isn't awesome because of the people you will gather around your table or the church family you get to worship with. What occurs today is a miracle—the sweetest of gifts from our good Father!

Today is a lot of reading, but try to take it in like it's the first time you've ever read it. Put yourself in the shoes of Jesus's followers as you read this story. They thought He was dead.

We are going to read a little, then process a little, then repeat. Hang with me. Read in awe of what your Father has done.

Read John 20:1-10

> **_» Who were the first ones to go to the tomb? What do you know about them?_**

> **_» What did they discover?_**

» What do you think they thought when they showed up? What would've been your first reaction?

The grave was empty. Jesus was not there but His grave clothes were—ruling out grave robbers or even Jesus's followers taking Him. I get a kick out of the fact that the clothes were folded. We don't know for sure who folded them or how the grave clothes came off Jesus. There are all kinds of theories, but they will remain theories until Heaven. At some point between when that grave stone was rolled closed and this moment we find ourselves, just two days later, Jesus had risen!

I wonder about this time often. How long did Jesus stay in the tomb? How long was he dead? How did those grave clothes get unraveled from Him? Who took the time to fold them? Why would they do that? How did the stone move? So many unknowns, and that's OK. We don't need to understand it all; it's part of God being God and us being man. We know only in part now, and that's good for us.

Ok, let's keep going. The women (we presume women even though only Mary is named because she says "we") were still at the grave site even though Peter and John had gone home.

Read John 20:11-18

» What emotion did Mary have? Why do you think she expressed this?

» Who did she see, and what did they say?

Her concern was for Jesus and where they could've taken Him. She was so concerned she didn't even seem afraid when she encountered angels. Most of the time, the presence of angels scared people, and they had to say, "Do not fear." Mary was so distracted with wanting to find Jesus that she didn't react to seeing not one but two angels. Then she missed something even bigger!

» Who showed up? Why do you think He chose this moment to reveal Himself? What does that tell you about Jesus?

He told her not to cling to Him and He told her to go, and that's just what she did. Can you imagine? The one you love and cherish and follow is alive! He isn't gone, and you are finally with Him again. Then all you get is just a moment. I don't know if I would've gone so quickly to tell the others. I would've wanted more time, not knowing what was going to happen.

Read John 20:19-23

> **» Who did He appear to next? Where?**

> **» What did He say when He was with them?**

Read John 20:24-29

> **» Who had yet to see Christ? What would make him believe?**

> **» How did Jesus prove Himself?**

> **» What does this teach you about believing in God?**

The story continues, even though our study ends here.

Have more time or need something for tomorrow? Keep reading in John and you can read what final lessons Jesus gave His disciples in John 21. Flip to another gospel and read when He gave them a final charge in Matthew 28:16-20. Then continue on into Acts and read about His Ascension and the first days of the early church.

> **» Read Matthew 5:14-16 and write out verse 14 below:**

LIGHT ALL SEVEN CANDLES

We light all the candles now because Christ has risen! We light all the candles now to remind ourselves that Jesus Himself called us the light of the world, and it's our turn to show people. Just as the early church did in Acts, it's our turn to carry on the message of the empty tomb.

» What is the message of the empty tomb? What does it mean for you?

Easter is the only true story of redemption. Our sins were nailed with Jesus to that cross; they were the nails in His hands. He died so that we don't have to. What makes Him so unlike any other God is that He rose again! This resurrection wasn't just to show His power but to give us new life! The Bible often reminds us that, like Jesus, we let our old selves die. Then we live a whole new life. Not a double life, a new life. What used to be is no longer. Our sin, our shame is no more. Jesus already paid that cost for you. Sure, sin still has consequences, but it doesn't bring condemnation.

New life. New Hope.

» Thank God for what He has done for you. Marvel in His amazing work of raising Jesus and us!

WHAT SHOULD I DO?

How can you apply what you have heard today? (James 1:22)

_____

_____

_____

WHO SHOULD I TELL?

What is something you can share about today? Who should you share this with?

_____

_____

_____

SHARE WHAT GOD IS TEACHING YOU!

Appendix

FOR GROUPS AND GROUP LEADERS

We were meant to live in connection and community with others. Let's gather together in groups to encourage, learn, listen, share, laugh, pray, and be women who are for one another during our holidays, and all the ordinary days in between.

Our hope is that we have a group (or more) meeting in each city in the United States. We know this is a crazy time of year for you but this is something that is so worth your time!

For more information on Groups, go to: sacredholidays.com/join-a-group

If you are interested in hosting a group, we think you are so awesome! We have a private Facebook group to support you, plus all kinds of free downloads to help you make your group awesome.

To sign your group up, go to: sacredholidays.com/host-a-group

Meet Becky Kiser

Becky is committed to seeing women fall in love with God's Word, then feel equipped and empowered to live it out. She believes that women can experience their own wild story, just like we see in the lives of God's chosen in His Word, as they love Jesus and love people. She is the founder and CEO of Sacred Holidays—a ministry dedicated to helping women find less chaos and more Jesus during holidays, engaging them through Bible study, community, resources, and lots of fun! She is determined to help women keep all the whimsy of the holidays, while making them sacred—holy and set apart. Her first book, *Sacred Holidays: Less Chaos, More Jesus,* was released with Lifeway and is available wherever books are sold online and in Lifeway stores. She has a background in marketing, ministry, and is a certified Myers-Briggs life coach, and she brings each of those experiences into her writing and speaking. Becky and her husband, Chris, live in The Woodlands, Texas, with their three girls.

Beckykiser.com | @beckykiser | facebook.com/becky.kiser

Meet the Lent Study Team

KELLY BOSCH | LEADER OF GROUPS

Kelly wholeheartedly believes we are better together. In her mind, life is bolder and brighter when done with others. She is passionate about creating connections through shared experiences and authentic hospitality. Jesus modeled it, and Kelly thinks we should live it out. She gathers people together – whether around a decorated table, over pizza and paper plates, or in a social media group – because she believes every single person deserves to have a seat at the table. We all have a story to tell and she wants to know yours. While around her table, you can expect to hear about her love of story and her fondness for the Marvel Cinematic Universe. She is a lady geek, sports fanatic, adventure seeker, and expert gift giver. Her affection runs deep for smoked brisket, potatoes of any kind, cupcakes, and all things coconut. Kelly lives in the State of Hockey (also known as Minnesota) with her hard-working husband, Jeff, and energetic sons, Xander & Gavin.

facebook.com/kellynbosch | @kellynbosch

MOLLY PARKER | EDITOR

Molly Parker is a copywriter and content editor who gets a kick out of words. Her fascination with clever storylines and catchy phrasing began the moment she flipped open *Gone With the Wind* in the eleventh grade. Helping clients craft engaging, personality-packed content ranks right up there with boxes of hand-picked See's Candies and cozy T.V. nights. Molly calls Southern California home with her grown-up kids, hunky husband, and sassy cat.

@mollyjeanparker | mollyjeanparker.com

MEGAN SJUTS WITH BUILDING 07 | STUDY DESIGNER

Megan Sjuts is the owner of Building 07 and designer for Sacred Holidays. Her mission as a designer is to simplify the design process and serve creative professionals and business owners. Building 07 offers a full range of professional design services that cover the gamut of graphic to web design, and all the creative strategy in between.

When she is not behind the screen designing for clients, she is teaching graphic design courses at Rogue Community College in Southern Oregon, where she lives with her husband, Elliot, their chocolate lab, Dixie, and four chickens, Sunny, Popcorn, Peanut, and Penny.

@building07 | Building07.com

WE GIVE 10% TO VULNERABLE WOMEN AND CHILDREN IN KENYA WITH OUR PARTNER, HIS VOICE GLOBAL

His Voice Global (HVG) is called to work in areas of the world with high populations of vulnerable women and children to partner with local leaders to fulfill their vision to care for, educate, and encourage the vulnerable women and children in their area. We currently have partnerships in South Sudan, Kenya, and Uganda.

Sacred Holidays specifically partners with our work in Kenya. HVG works in a city in which prostitution and the commercial sex trade industry dominates the economy. Women and children, both by force and by choice, work the streets in order to feed and house themselves and their children. We are partnered with a local Kenyan church called Rift Valley Fellowship (RVF). RVF staff works tirelessly to help these women and children get off the streets and into affordable homes and integrity filled jobs. We have a boys and a girls home, providing holistic restoration including safety, education, counseling, and over all physical care. As children come into our care, we work closely with their mothers through a ministry to the women called Women of Courage. Women of Courage exist to love, provide, disciple, and train women in trades that they can eventually support themselves.

HOW YOU CAN HELP!

First, you already have! You purchasing this study has provided funds for this work!

- ☐ If you'd like to do more, there are so many ways you can help advocate for these beautiful women and children in Kenya.

- ☐ Educate yourself. Hear the stories and the needs. Follow His Voice Global on social media: @hisvoiceglobal and facebook.com/hisvoice. Also, learn lots more and sign up for our newsletter so that you can grow as an advocate for these vulnerable women and children in Kenya at www.hisvoiceglobal.com

- ☐ Support a child by giving them an education: For an Elementary and Middle School study it is $165 a year, or just $14 a month. For High School students it's $600 a year, or $50 a month. This sacrifice on your part is what will change the future of that kid's life!

- ☐ Support a mother as she chooses to stay off the streets: $135 a month to provide a home, food, hygiene items, clothing, and job support.

- ☐ Provide a week worth of food for our feeding program that keeps kids from working the street in order to eat. It also pays to feed everyone in the Recovery program on Saturdays and anyone who comes to church on Sunday, often their only meal/meals of the weekend. $170 a week. We know this is a larger expense, so grab a few friends and go into this together if this isn't something you could do on your own.

☐ Sign up to go to Kenya or Uganda with our teams! Contact amber@ hisvoiceglobal.com for more information on our trips.

☐ Become a monthly partner of His Voice Global! There are countless needs that come up to support the work being done in Kenya. By giving generally you allow there to be resources for the local church to meet the needs of the people as they arise.

☐ Host an advocacy night in your home. Grab 10 or so (or more!) of your friends and host a night in your home where they can learn about His Voice Global. We will provide you with video or a staff member to come and share. This can look any way you want it! You can have it low key or super to-do! During the halftime of a big game, or an entire dinner and program. Contact amber@ hisvoiceglobal.com and she will make it happen! We can brainstorm together what would be the most fun and best fit for your people.

P.S. from Becky

Ladies, I cannot encourage you enough to do something, anything. I endorse very few ministries because I want you to know the things I push you to be a part of are worth your time, doing real work, and being good stewards of your funds. I have been to Kenya now twice and have known Amber and Vernon, the founders of this ministry for nearly two decades— they and this ministry are the real deal. I have stood in the homes of women who were once prostituting themselves all throughout the day just to provide a bite to eat for the week for their family. But God. He has used HVG and RVF to bring about His redemption story.

FOLLOW HIS VOICE GLOBAL ON SOCIAL MEDIA!

Instagram: @hisvoiceglobal | Facebook: His Voice Global

SACRED HOLIDAYS: LESS CHAOS, MORE JESUS
BY BECKY KISER

Available where books are sold online and in LifeWay Stores:

LET'S REALLY STAY FRIENDS

Sacredholidays.com // facebook.com/sacredholidays // facebook.com/groups/SacredHolidaysTribe // @sacredholidays

We love you so much, I hope you've heard that throughout this study. We want, more than anything else, to come alongside you during these chaotic and magical holidays and help you know Christ and love others more!

Chat with you soon!

Love you! Mean it.

Becky Kiser + the Sacred Holidays Team

Made in the USA
Monee, IL
11 November 2020